Write Dance

A Progressive Music and Movement Programme for the Development of Pre-writing and Writing skills in children

for Ariane

by Ragnhild Oussoren Voors

Ragnhild Oussoren Voors was born in Holland and is of mixed Norwegian and Dutch descent. She has lived many years in Scandinavia but also in Belgium and in France. She has a degree in Graphology (writing psychology) and received her training in France and in Holland. Ragnhild has long experience of working with children, both in groups and individually.

The Write Dance method was developed during the late eighties and early nineties in close collaboration with schools and preschools in Sweden.

Since the Write Dance method was first published in 1993 in Sweden, the author has moved to the Netherlands (www.Schrijfdans.nl). Write Dance part two was written in 1995 and both parts are now published in Denmark, Germany, the Netherlands and Sweden. An additional volume will be published in the Netherlands early in 2000.

Today more than 500,000 children are Write-Dancing daily.

Write Dance aims to develop students' coordination skills through a combination of movements, dance, music and drawing. Write Dance attempts to make this connection through a series of sessions that combine a response to music, large-scale movements and the development of fine motor coordination.

Write Dance is both body-dance and a written interplay of lines. It may be offered as a writing lecture, a drawing, music, or a physical lesson.

The purpose of Write Dance is to let the child develop a personal, rhythmic and legible handwriting, resulting in a fluent, flowing and flexible handwriting.

ISBN 1 873 94203 6

Contents

May I have the pleasure of a Write Dance?

Write Dance is a movement-based method of training children's fine and gross coordination and as a result ending up with comfortable, readable, quick and distinctive hand writing. Today about 35,000 Swedish children use the Write Dance method and its use is increasing in many other European countries.

On training days I met a lot of enthusiasm for the method among teachers but until now a programme for regular application hasn't existed. I created this programme with a lot of joy and enthusiasm, from students as well as from teachers, and it's now used in pre-schools and junior schools.

In Write Dance part one, we are not using the letters in our play but we use the shapes of the letters, i.e. the basic movements. In the 9 themes included in part one, the children will, in a creative and playful way, practise all the movements, the pressure, and the speed that together make up our letters. In these exercises the children will find rhythm and energy in their coordination and a future joy in writing. This is important and effective even for older children with difficult writing problems.

Music plays a central role or rather as central as the children and you allow. The children love the music and recognise the support and inspiration it gives. The music is the motor that starts the body and the intellect. After a while the children will automatically and unconsciously start their own internal motor to find a rhythm. Then we will have succeeded.

Movement also has a central role in Write Dance. When we learn to walk one would think that the steps are the most important but that is not so. It is the movement that must come before the step. And it is just like that in writing. It is easy to just look at the individual letters and their shapes, when at first, it is the movement and the rhythm that is most important.

Rhymes have always been important to humans. Write Dance integrates this fact. For all 9 themes there is a rhyme with movements suitable for just that theme. Here we use the voice as a rhythm instrument.

To integrate writing into the whole body develops a good body-balance and gives the child a relationship to the letters. Because of this it is important to give the children a chance to write with their whole body, to integrate the basic movements into their body. Write Dance gives opportunities for them to do that.

In the past people wrote beautifully but slowly, with discipline and with more or less individual style. Time has changed and now it is more important to write fast and legibly (but not necessarily beautifully). To have a will to write the hand must feel comfortable and that happens when the writing is elastic and full of energy.

These days writing has only one function: to establish and make visual our intellectual thoughts and efforts. The technique and the time pressure have suppressed the writing artist within us. Writers and artists still often write by hand and experience not only joy but also inspiration when doing so; the movement in itself activates the body and the brain.

It is generally recognised that creativity and development must start with the person . Handwriting is a very personal and creative form of expression that mustn't be lost to us. But it shouldn't just come from the fingers but grow from within us and this is best done by this method because:
…abstract movements become concrete lines!

My own daughter, Ariane, has, since she was two, been part of all these experiments that resulted in the Write Dance. Schools and pre-schools around Stockholm have been very involved in the development of the methods. A big thanks to you all.

Write Dance has a very clear holistic view of the growing and learning human so again, remember to integrate the method in many subjects.

Good luck.

Ragnhild O Voors

What is Write Dance?

Write Dance is a method that integrates the whole body in the development of coordination of hands and fingers. With the aid of imaginative drawing, music, rhymes, rhythm and games the conditions for a flowing and joined-up hand are created. An understanding is created of the interdependence between the body movements and small hand/finger movements. The abstract movements are turned into cursive lines.

Write Dance also trains the children to survey the writing page (and to dare go across it), to use crayon/pen-movements at different speeds and energy and develops a feel for relations between the different letter shapes.

Through the body-coordinating exercises the children are trained to balance the body, the eyes and the two brain-halves. This should lead to a better physical and psychological health and to a feeling of joy about learning to write and writing itself.

Write Dance is a method based on experiences gained in the writing psychology that was developed in France at the end of the 19th century, and writing-teaching which has its roots in Germany around 1960.

What is writing psychology?

Handwriting is defined as: the "track that remains on the page after the act of writing". All research about handwriting and its possible usefulness as a psycho-diagnostic tool, belong to psychology". (Teut Wallner, author of 'From graphology to writing psychology', Seminarium Publishers)

Until just recently this science has above all been used by recruitment firms, inside psychiatry and in connection with criminal investigations. Recently writing psychology, in the form of writing pedagogy, has started to be used in schools in Germany and Holland.

In the 1940's, Berlion (France) discovered, by using writing psychological exercises, that patients with smaller or larger psychological problems, improved by grapho-therapeutic exercises. Magdalene Heerman in Germany did research in the 1960's together with a psychiatrist. Many children, even those with serious psychological damage, made improvements within a year.

Heerman is the first graphologist who has created a writing pedagogical method, called Schreib Bewegenungsterapie. Much of Magdalene Heermann's knowledge and experience is to be found in the Write Dance method.

Teaching writing in Sweden in the 1990s?

The so called SÖ style, published in 1972, was never a success, neither for teachers or children. An investigation found that "three quarters of pupils leaving school have a clear and easily read hand writing, but most of them are printing half or even the whole text". (From the Curriculum for Handwriting, 1989)

An investigation shows that Primary school children practise writing for, on average 35 minutes per week and junior school children on average 30 minutes. This is far too little. It should be 15-20 minutes per school day! The SÖ style has been sharply criticised by writing psychological groups. With it's functional construction, its inconsistent physiological unsuitability or by the shapes' difficult linkage, it demands such a high concentration that a relaxed and physiologically natural movement is excluded. (Lennart Bergstom, Consultation Paper - 1972)

Handwriting, SÖ style, printing style….What should we do now? Sweden's writing pedagogy is in a very critical situation. The Education Department has not published any new proposal for a recommended style but lets each teacher decide how to do it. Neither does Education Department say anything about handwriting as an important daily subject. This is most unfortunate. To learn to swim we must learn how to move our arms and legs. To learn to write we must in the same way learn the movements so we can stay afloat on the paper.

Practise play and games with the writing movements every day, for coordination, for joy and confidence and creativity. A child's self confidence is reflected in its writing.

Better results are achieved by children who have a regular daily gross motor exercise programme, such as is described in for instance 'Full fart i livet' by Gustavsson/Hugo.

hedgehogs frogs and slugs

hedgehogs frogs and slugs

How is the Write Dance programme organised?

The Write Dance method part 1, contains 9 different themes. With these nine themes the children will practise all the movements and lines in our written letters.

Every theme has a special movement exercise that is trained, played with and worked on by gross and fine coordination exercises.

With every theme comes a special piece of music, working as a support and help for the children when it comes to finding the movement, the speed and the tension. The music is used to advantage when the child "does Write Dance with their whole body". This means that if the theme is "the Growing Tree" it can be an advantage to start in the play area/gym and with the help of the music and the body create and shape the tree from the inside and from the outside of ourselves.

There is also a rhyme with every theme. With the rhyme there are exercises for the whole body or just for hands and fingers (if you prefer to sit down).

Every theme has its own imaginative music drawing. With the theme "the Volcano" it is of course a volcano that, with the help of the music, should be created on the surface. A good way to start is to stand up and become a volcano, with body and soul.

Apart from the "musicdrawing" there are many drawing exercises with every theme. Some are most suitable for individual work, others for work in pairs or small groups.

A lot of work is done with an blindfold. (Practical explanations, tips and ideas, page 20) The blindfold increases the experience of written movements and self-confidence.

To have the different Write Dance exercises as part of lessons every day is ideal. The teacher should plan for this in the day's programme. Motor training has a positive effect on concentration and develops creativity, enjoyment and, last but by no means least, a readable, individual and rhythmic joined up writing. A happy child is a harmonious child.

How much time one theme should take is of course very variable. It depends on the size of the group, how interested they are and how well developed. There is a lot to do. Generally it is better to Write Dance often for short periods than for longer less often. The more of Write Dance that can be integrated in other subjects, the better.

The aim is to make the children well developed in their movements in a natural and playful way. Learning the basic forms of the letters and how they are joined, presented in Write Dance part 2, will then feel logical and writing becomes an automatic process with less hang ups, frustrations and disturbing 'scrawls'.

Write Dance 2 is very like Write Dance 1. The music plays an important role here as well, helping the children to find a soft, rolling and fast writing style. The letters are trained and played with, as well as the base movements.

At what age should Write Dance be introduced?

Write Dance part 1 is developed for children from 5 to 8. Many years' experience has shown that the material and the method is excellent for older children and teenagers with severe writing difficulties, as well.

It is never too late to start gross motor exercises. But to practise regularly is more difficult for adults than the exercises per se.

Many young adults, particularly men, are dissatisfied with their handwriting mainly because they didn't get enough practise in handwriting at school. Technological machines, telephones, adding machines, computers with their keyboards means that handwriting is used less and less. But the more seldom handwriting is used, the less movements are practised and the style gets worse. In the end the keyboard is all that is left. It is obvious that this moves the development away from readable, quick and joined-up writing.

In year 1 the teaching of reading happens together with the learning of letters and numbers. During the period when a child still hasn't learnt to read they should train the very important writing movements. This is particularly important for boys and children with weak coordination.

In year 1-4 children can use the fine and gross motor exercises since the teachers pedagogy at this point still hasn't implemented a general writing programme. Experience shows that children up till 11 years old can learn to handwrite nicely, and for girls even later is possible.

School education is, in the main, aiming at developing intellectual ability but the writing ability comes from the child's own internal artistry and creativity - and by developing the ability to write (the logical form of letters) self confidence is increased.

Improvement of handwriting in secondary school happens by the initiative and motivation of the teenagers themselves. Many boys at that age have problems with their handwriting even if they don't want to own up to this. When they must write clearly and legibly, it takes far too long and feels very uncomfortable. The writing becomes unreadable. Most teenagers have forgotten or never practised enough the basic movements. They often experiment with illogical, wrong or difficult solutions to avoid joining up difficult letters.

By Write Dance training the children develop a better idea of the body and a feel for the whole. The result of this is:

Better relation between letter forms, movement and distribution.

Form	Movement	Distribution
form *form*	*mouvement* *Mouvement*	*distribution* *distribution*

Better distribution within the letter:
like risers and descenders in relation to the medium zone.

over zone
middle zone   *writing   writing   writing*
under zone

not like this   **not like this**   **like this!**

9

Is the Write Dance method tied to any prescribed style?

Write Dance is not tied to any prescribed style. The idea is that the children themselves can choose, with a well-developed coordination, from their own logical movements and from their own personality.

The quicker a child starts joining-up letters, the better, says Torbjorn Danielsen. This provided the child's coordination is adequate/satisfactory.

Danielsen was appointed by the Norwegian Education Department to do research on the development of children's handwriting. The project took place between 1976 and 1979 and he reports the result in a detailed book "The Brain and letter formation".

His way of seeing the brain's functions in relation to letter formation is a development of the graphologist Pophal's ideas (1950) Handschrift-Hirnschrift (Hand-and Brain writing). Danielsen's report is an important step in the writing psychological study about handwriting in relation to the teaching of writing.

His main thesis is as follows: Parents and teachers are on firm ground if they choose looped writing for their children (The SÖ style has no looped letters).

Torbjörn Danielsen is a psychologist and a writing psychologist specialising in neuro-pedagogy, a teacher and a reader at a Norwegian Teacher Training College, and a leading expert on basic motor learning of writing.

He says that it is about time that we now have large scale trials of a method to teach mother tongue that is not based on writing in printed style. The Swedish SÖ style is the same as the Norwegian so-called *"form and stave style"* (from the 1950's) something he has fought for many years. In 1989 his ideas were approved by the Norwegian Education Department. The stylised formal type of writing is now being overtaken by looped writing in Norway. We see the same tendency in Sweden today.

Why does one person generally write better than others?

Many boys hate writing. They don't have the patience, get irritated easily and in time, build up a fear of writing. It is very common for them to keep this fear even as adults. They fight the handwriting's current instead of floating with it. They haven't learnt the basic movements that lead to logical joining, in a rhythmic way.

Girls generally write better than boys. The reason for this is physiological and deeply psychological, in body and soul.

More than half of the letters are shaped out of round forms. Round movements are feminine; girls dance, skip around, and hug each other.

Boys on the other hand, compete with each other, shoot at a goal, slap each other's backs. The movements of boys tend to be stretched, straight and angled.

Writing has been developed so we can express thoughts and communicate. We communicate from ourselves to someone else, from the left to the right. According to the principles of writing psychology the "I" is on the left and the "you" is on the right (in our culture).

When they have problems women help each other by talking, confessing, crying, writing down, telling each other and listening. The symbol for this is the round garland (an 'n' written as a 'u'). Garland forms are very popular with around puberty girls. This can be a proof of skilled coordination.

Straight lines have the angle as basic form. This is needed as support and to structure our handwriting but we often see far too many angles in boys' writing because they are not able to use round forms. The pressure on the paper and the grip on the pen are both hard and the style uncomfortable. The round forms that link our letters are not there and the writing lacks the energy and softness needed. The handwriting is clumsy and stiff instead.

But remember:
- Writing consists of both round and straight lines.
- Both are needed.
- We need to practise both

To keep the body healthy you must move, jump, run and practice your movements. Why should it be different when it comes to our psycho-motor most personal and artistic expression, our handwriting?

The teaching principles of Write Dance.

Straight and round are the basic movements and the basic forms in our letters and figures.

1. Straight forms/lines have the characteristic of being tense and firm and belong together with rhythm and counting, Straight lines have a tendency to firm forms and of being slow.

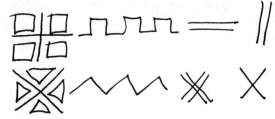

2. Round forms have the characteristic of being soft and relaxed. They belong together with melody and flexibility. Round lines have a tendency to soft forms and flow faster than straight lines. Picture here

3. Circle movements can go left or right. We write from left to right but our letters contain circle movements to the left as well.

The arcade is developed by circle movements, starting to the right.

The garland is developed by circle movements, starting to the left.

4. The angled movement.

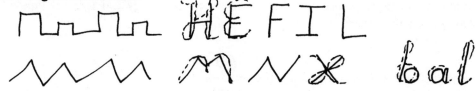

5. All these basic movements are practised and played with in Write Dance.

It is very effective to practise these in four different directions.

The children can do this when they know all the themes well. Helped by the music, for instance, the Train, the Robot and the Silverwings.

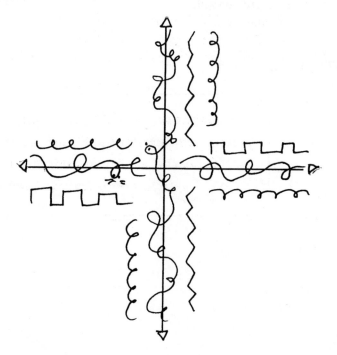

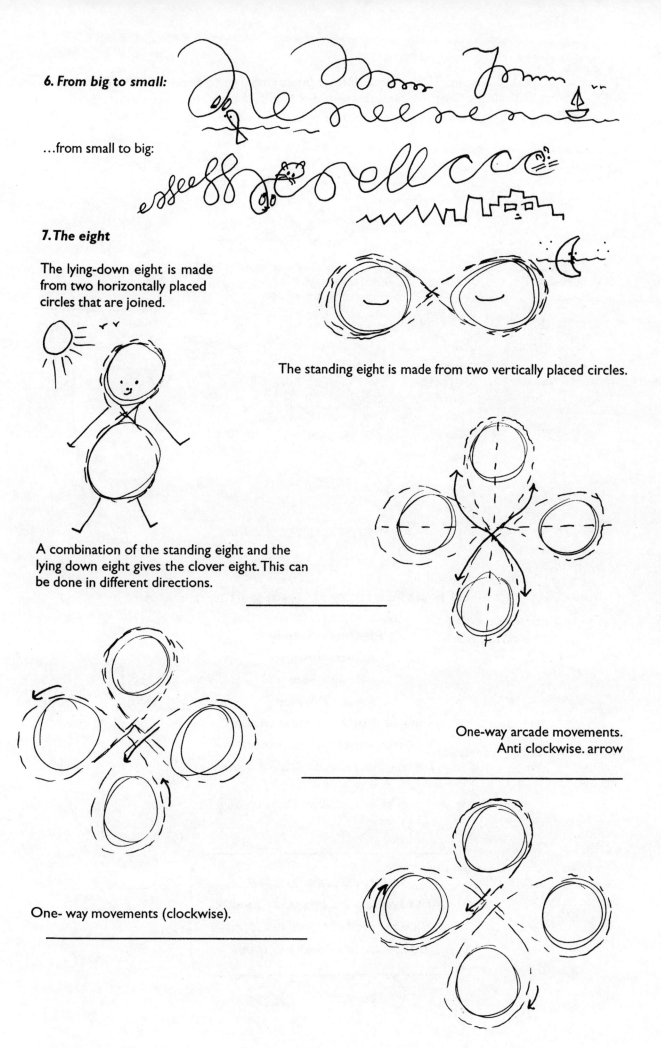

6. From big to small:

...from small to big:

7. The eight

The lying-down eight is made from two horizontally placed circles that are joined.

The standing eight is made from two vertically placed circles.

A combination of the standing eight and the lying down eight gives the clover eight. This can be done in different directions.

One-way arcade movements.
Anti clockwise. arrow

One-way movements (clockwise).

...or via a cross movement. This is more difficult but a challenge to brain- eye- hand- coordination. Practice creates balance. Create the leaves alternately in pairs, like eighths.

The aim of Write Dance is, by rhythmic practice, to combine:

Rhythm - Melody
Intellect - Emotion
Body - Soul
Tense - Relaxed
Sense motor - Psycho motor
Gross motor - Fine motor
Form - Movement - Distribution

...see The Write Dance Daisy on page 26

Letters are sound symbols
Sound symbols are created by humans
Humans are body, soul and spirit
Letters are body, soul and spirit.

Letters can be compared and divided up just like the human body (according to Pulver.)

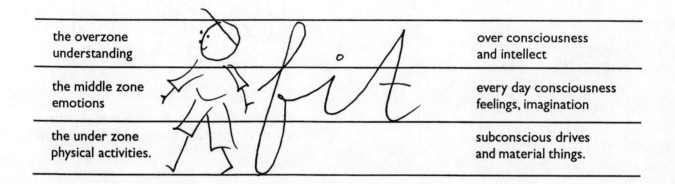

the overzone understanding	over consciousness and intellect
the middle zone emotions	every day consciousness feelings, imagination
the under zone physical activities.	subconscious drives and material things.

Symbolism

Concepts like upwards, downwards just like right and left have played a very important part in the development of human culture. Our way of thinking is permeated by these concepts and symbols. We use them consciously also even when we write.

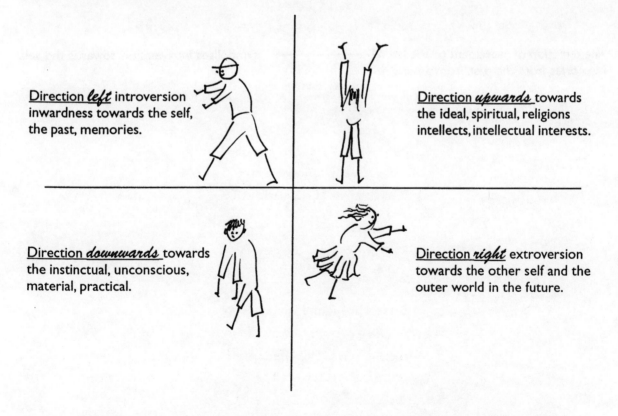

Direction *left* introversion inwardness towards the self, the past, memories.

Direction *upwards* towards the ideal, spiritual, religions intellects, intellectual interests.

Direction *downwards* towards the instinctual, unconscious, material, practical.

Direction *right* extroversion towards the other self and the outer world in the future.

(According to Pulver one of the first graphologists to introduce this as a theory)

We talk of high moral principles -
they go upwards. People feel
elated.

We speak of low instincts of low objectives.
The bottom is reached. People say they feel down.

Further, the rightwards direction symbolises ————————▷ extroversion.

In the Western world we write from left to
right. After a few seconds words that are
written are already in the past. I write from
myself to you. The self lies on the left, the
other lies on the right. From left to right is
also the direction towards the outer world and
the future. The way towards what we are
striving after. Our distant goals and intentions.
Our thoughts, hopes.

The direction of movement to the left ◁———————— symbolises introversion, towards the self.
Memories from the past, from an origin.

The rhythm of handwriting

occurs in connection with gross and fine motor and psychomotor movements of expression:

tense, relaxed, form, movement distribution. up, down, right, left.

The rhythm of handwriting can be positive formed from balanced and rhythmic movements. It can be negative when it's in imbalance and arrhythmical.

We get positive writing by practising gross-, fine-, sensory-, and psychomotor activities. This is valuable as a positive handwriting creates self-esteem. Intuitively we often interpret people's body language as stiff, tense, sloppy. In the same way, sometimes unconsciously, we interpret the handwriting as well.

Look at the following handwriting styles; think about them and discuss whether each is a harmonious and rhythmical handwriting or unharmonic and arrhythmical.

+Practical Explanation - Ideas and Tips

Material:

- CD player.
- <u>Big piece of paper</u>: preferably A3 or larger. It can be wall paper or rolls of paper. Working with big rolls of paper on the floor is excellent, for practising balance when one's kneeling. Make sure that the children don't sit too near each other because they get stuck together and don't have any freedom of movement.
- <u>Coloured chalks</u>: not too long because they squeak, for younger children thicker chalks.
- <u>Coloured pens and brushes</u>: perhaps Indian Ink for touching up drawings afterwards.
- <u>Blind fold</u>: which can sometimes be used for music exercises, games and individual practice. Making movements without being able to see them deepens the experience of movement and opens new paths in the brain and to related feelings. This strengthens self esteem. You can find a pattern for blindfold on page 22.
- <u>Blue tac</u>: a pea sized bit for each child. Tip: for quick and well organised handing out it might be a good idea for each child to bring a bottle top from home and keep their bit of blue tac in it, all the bottle tops can then be kept by the teacher in a box. The bits of blue tac can also be stored on a piece of wood, perhaps divided up into little sections with each child's name, or picture on it.
- <u>Write Dance File</u>: let the children collect their materials together in a special file, it's very fruitful for the children to be able to look back to their earlier drawings and exercises to think about whether anything's changed.
- <u>Masonite boards</u>: These can be sawed up into suitable sizes, 100 x 60cms or perhaps less, and used as tables. Paint them once with matt paint and then they'll be a bit like blackboards. You can buy anti-allergic chalk as well. These will then make quite cheap material which can easily be used for floor, table or wall placements for practising both horizontal and vertical writing positions. Cut a sponge into 6 pieces. Each child uses a pair.

Some concepts: from the french writing psychology of writing come the concepts of;

arcades or bows

garlands or waves.

Explain to the children that arcade means a bow or loop, and garland means a party-garland. Try to make this clear, arcades for example with Romanesque church buildings and therefore garlands like the things we hang up at parties, like you see on a flag pole or on boats, or bowls of sweets.

Music:

Each theme has its own music on CD.

Start by practising the movements in the air with both hands, this helps lateralisation. And many left handed children discover which is the correct hand. being left handed doesn't have to be a disadvantage for writing. After these exercises in the air go straight on to draw them on paper which you have already stuck down to the tables. At first you can repeat the music drawings directly over the previous one which reduces the fear of failure and strengthens the programming of the movements.

Special education teachers, day-care staff and parents.

As groups and classes get bigger and the staffing more sparse it is important to be able to involve as many people as possible in children's development.   Parents ought to be helped to understand what it's about, and what its purpose is, and perhaps they could also join in at home or at school.

It's a good idea to spread the Write Dance lessons out, make them shorter but more frequent. Do the gross movement in the gym or play hall, and then go back to your normal room and do the movements and the rhymes in the air and after that the same big movements on paper.

On the big board one or two children may want to be put up by the board to experience even greater freedom of movements and to practise the movements against a vertical background. The more you practise on different types of surface - horizontal, the table, vertical, the blackboard etc. the better it is for eye hand coordination.

To do something on the blackboard in front of the whole group can be frightening for the shy or it can be quite nervy for the brave. Since it's a question of movement pictures, and it isn't about creating shapes, everything is personal and it's all correct. Just for once there's no picture which has to be made exactly like the model, so the risk and therefore the fear of failure is reduced. Sponges are useful to discover movement and lines with one or two hands. This is especially important for children with poor co-ordination.

Everybody can work freely, it's not intended that the results on the big blackboard are supposed to be a model for the rest of the children. Depending on the teacher's own imagination interest each weekly theme can be handled in lots of different ways and integrated in many different subjects.

A theme can be used in other games as well, for example everybody sits round in a circle blindfolded. Let different figures, pictures, forms pass round the group, the children have to investigate the things, they're round, soft, straight, hard, sharp - what sort of things fit in with this week's theme.

Maybe the children can even show particular characteristics and forms with their bodies, this is a very suitable exercise for preschool. The more you get inside the theme the more possibilities for games you'll discover.

The first exercise, the volcano, can lead to a rather chaotic atmosphere in the group because we do encourage the children to make big movements. The music is very stimulating and inspiring, and it may therefore be an advantage to start just with half the group.

The music, 'a Walk in the country' and 'Silver wings over the sea' create a rather calmer atmosphere and there are rarely problems, even with big groups. Practical way of organising, all this depends of course on the size of the group, their maturity and their age. After a while children realise that it isn't just a game, but there is a certain discipline required as well.

Blindfolds

1 Copy the patterns, the shapes in A and B separately.

2 Make a suitable number of patterns to cut around of each size in cardboard, and give them out to the children.

3 Shape A is cut out in coarse drawing paper, shape B is cut out in cloth.

4 Fold the cloth round the paper shape A and stick it down. Make 2 slots for the nose, and if you want you can stick another model A on the back of the blindfold to avoid rubbing and stray bits of cloth and wrinkles.

5 Cut out 22cms long piece of elastic for each blindfold, make a knot in each end and fix it on with a stapler using the sharp bits outwards.

6 Let the children decorate their blindfolds - painting, glueing shapes on etc.

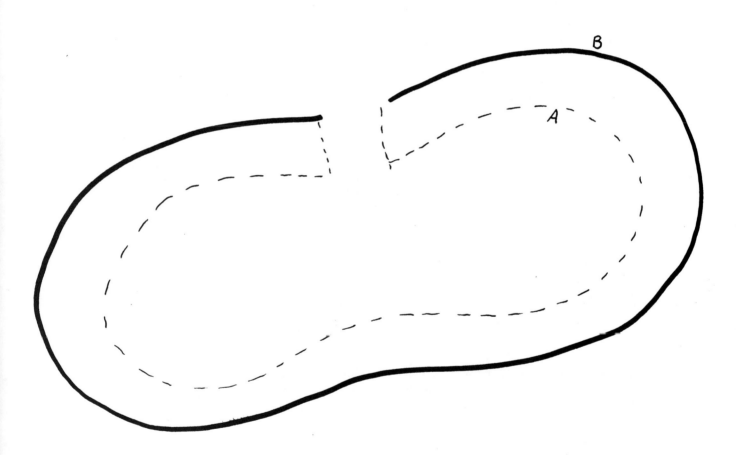

—The writing movement test.

We know from experience that children like this kind of test a lot, and that they haven't yet developed a fear of failure, because this is only about writing movements and not about intellectual achievements.

The idea of the test above all is that the children themselves should be able to see their own progress or recognise their own fine motor problems; in that case children can practise these at after school club or at home, helped by their parents. The quicker that you give extra writing help the better, this reduces the risk for irritation, frustration, repeated failure while developing a handwriting style.

The test which here is for school children is best done:
> before you begin Write Dance
> between weeks 5 and 6
> and after week 9.

For younger children or children with special needsa similar test can be done with lines and movements which are known to that particular age or group.

So do it like this:
- Give out a copy of lined paper, from the next page. The distance of the lines is an A4 folded in 8 sections.
- Describe and demonstrate the tasks in the air, let children copy you. You might want to do 4 - 7 on the blackboard as well.

The figures are to be drawn on the rows or in the sections.

1- a long straight line

2 - draw 5 circles

3 - draw 5 circular rings
   Demonstrate in the air

4 - upwards loops, garlands

5 - downwards loops, arcades

6 - do mountain tops

7 - draw 5 eights

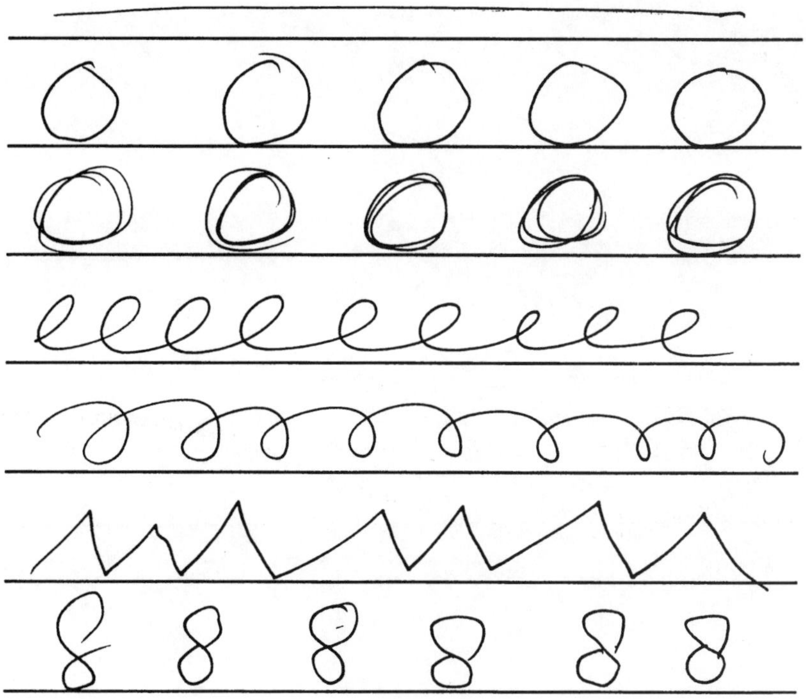

8 - just draw - let the
   imagination of the child grow.

Maria Heppner demonstrates in her book Schlussel zur Kinderschrift (The Key to Children's Handwriting) the connection between children's written expression of movements and their psyche and personality. This can be read out from the three basic movements arcades, garlands and angles.

The book, which is only available in German is very interesting and comprehensive, Interested readers will find here a very good comprehensive overview/complete picture of psychology of writing. These writing pedagogical principles are the basis for this writing movement test.

Apart from factors which could temporarily interfere with the test results, for example particular time, a child's physical and psychic state etc., you can nearly always see clear fine motor development between the three test periods. If there is significant deterioration it is obviously a good idea to check the child's general health and particularly their eyes.

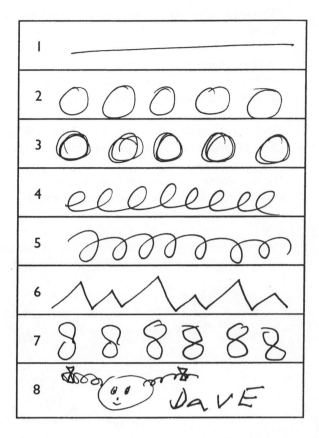

A brief interpretation of the writing movement test

Note that there are many variations here and only the most common have been interpreted.

1 A long, straight and powerful line, particularly from side to side, can signify vitality, ability to take an overview and purposefulness. A careful, hesitant and perhaps trembling line often from side to side can mean uncertain motor skills, with perhaps also sensibility, cautiousness, fear of failure, perfectionism and ambition and hardwork.

2 The division of the circles. It's quite normal for children to draw circles right next to each other, particularly towards the left (see the symbolism of the cross). The better the distribution of the circles the greater the ability is to take an overview, organisational ability and hand eye co-ordination.

3 The shape of the circle, the rounder and more regular the circle the more harmonious the child is both from the fine motor and the psychic point of view. Chaotic circles are found more commonly with boys than girls and these mean impatience, vitality, aggressiveness, a lack of concentration or perhaps just less concern for appearance.

The more open the circles are the more intellectual and emotional clarity and maturity the child is showing.

Children prefer proper circles around 5 to 6 years of age. At that time spontaneity is starting to develop into more intellectual interest.

Circles that are drawn too slowly and carefully and with an uncertain line, can be a sign of over-control, a fear of failure, a docility and tendency to work too hard.

These children need an extra amount of practice in their circular movements to avoid scrawl and cramped style.

Clear and well organised division, either of the page or of the line, can be an indication of flexibility in social contacts (see the symbolism of the cross).

4 Looped Garland

The form symbol is a boat form or bowl  and that means relaxed.

it means openness, spontaneity,  communications, social contacts.

5 Looped arcade

The form symbol is the bow or the arch form.

Tense upward and inward movements

it means a need for independence, active imagination and world of fantasy.

Children who can't or have difficulty with changing between garlands and the arcade movements maybe have slightly slow brain signals, or maybe difficulties with the bending and stretching muscles in the fingers, poorly developed motor abilities or maybe the visual ability to focus and be focused isn't sufficiently well-developed. However this is common around five/six years of age.

Generally, children learn these movements quickly. Give children a more associative name for the arcade, if the problem with the confusion continues, for example: you can talk about hopping movements for the arcade. You can illustrate it as a bow, as a tunnel, as hopscotch. The garland can be explained as either a bowl or a swing movement, illustrated with a bowl, scales or a swing. The more often you practise these two basic movements the more stimulation there is for both the halves of the brain and the eyes. This influences the flexibility and elasticity both in motor skills and in the psyche.

6 The Angle, the symbolic form is the change of direction -

Vitality. A resistance, an ability to work.

A copying ability, a concentration. Hard pressing and pointed angles can be an indication of negative, rather than positive, progression.

Sloppy, irregular and unclear corners can mean impatience, lack of concentration, a lack of ability to keep going.

7 <u>Eights</u>. 88888 A very complicated figure and movement, both for the eyes and the brain and therefore for the prime motor skills as a whole. Here it is important to interpret the division and the form of movement (see points 2 and 3). Some children already in Year 1 start to join

up their eights in regular movements, most often it's girls.

The theme circles and eights is an important exercise to the shape.

8 Choose one or more writing exercises: here the children can show their joy and cleverness in their fine motor skills. Draw, create. This is where imagination creativity is stimulated.

Training and practice of gross and fine motor writing movements always has a positive effect on the personality and character, quite apart from the fact that it's an important precondition or foundation for a rhythmic personal and legible handwriting, or fluent, flow and flexible!

The Oxeye Daisy. A balance with Write Dance.

Write Dance is aholistic approach and the effects of the method are summarised in the oxeye daisy below.

This flower might be suitable to have as a starting point for informing teachers, Senco's, parents etc. about Write Dance's aims and method.

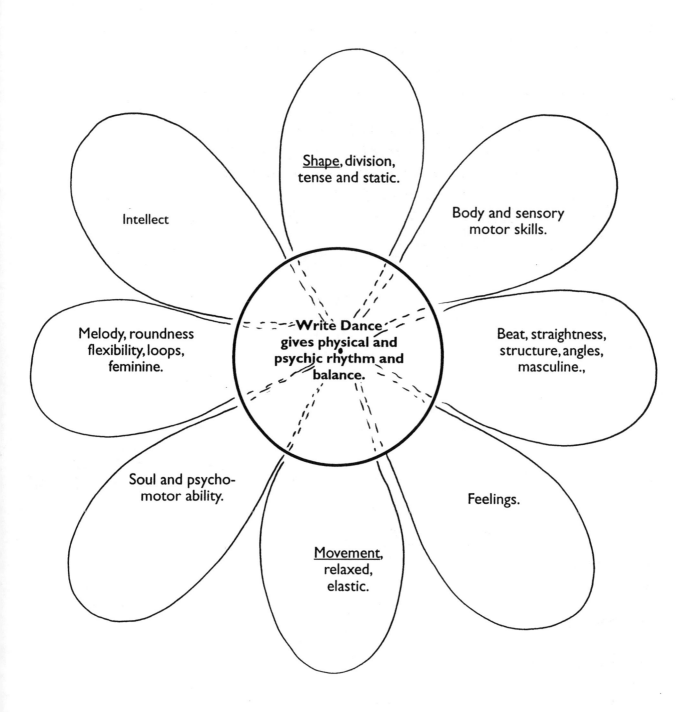

There are 4 pairs of eights. In a single movement, Oxeye Daisy is created.

Learning to write.

Learning to write is just like learning to dance. In order to be able to do a dance, whether it's a particular one, or just spontaneous, following the tones and rhythms of the music it's necessary to learn steps. It's not easy for everyone to keep their bodies in balance at the same time. The brain, muscles, nerves, arms and legs all have to work together in order to perform the dance that we've decided on. The more you practise, the better it goes. The smoother and more skilled the body, the more beautiful the dance is. Learning to write works in just the same way. Tiny movements that we see on the paper are, in fact, a dance. Although the body is still when we write, the muscles, nerves, thoughts and feelings are active all the time. Through body-movements the brain becomes programmed, precisely like a computer. Big body movements are converted into small dance steps, movement and playing with lines together will develop. That's why we talk about Write Dance.

So, before each step comes a movement. Write Dance is an explicitly movement focused method. Form is important, of course, but it is secondary. The primary thing is to find a flow and a rhythm in the handwriting and then, later, you can make small alterations to the actual form of the handwriting, the shapes.

The Write Dance daily practise

Start to tell the introductory story about the theme in your own words. Continue with fross motor movements in the gym, hall or classroom. At first without music, not too quick, then with music. Paper and boards are already prepared and stuck with blu tac on the table or on the floor. Continue with movements on the writing surface, selfmade board, wallpaper or large sheet of paper. Again, at first without music, then with music. Stop the music from time to time for discussions or corrections. Children preferable stand behind the table. Disabled children may sit down.

The psychomotorical effects of these themes.

The objective of Write Dance is to reach a fluent, flowing and flexible handwriting

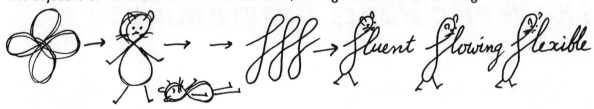

The Volcano,

A liberating feeling, an overview and division of a surface - warming up, heating. Stimulation of writing movements. An opportunity to talk about body and feelings. The Volcano practises the over and under loops of writing.

A Walk in the Country.

This is stimulating imagination and relaxing. It's an opportunity to talk about reality and dreams. It stimulates connections and harmony in writing.

Circles and eights, circles and eights.

It creates an atmosphere of peacefulness: It is stimulating cross movements for the eyes and the brain. Logical thinking. Problem and conflict solving. It stimulates flow in the writing movements.

Robot.

Warming up, bodily coordination. Independence and persistence. It reinforces assertiveness. It stimulates definite and clear angles in the writing.

The Train.

Stimulates opposite signals. It increases the speed of writing and practises links between letters. It develops a consciousness of breathing. The train develops loops in writing.

The Growing Tree.

This emphasises the basic, discipline and spontaneity, organisation and improvisation, bodily and written movement coordination. This exercise practises many of the basic movements of writing.

Silverwings over the Sea.

Consciousness of the difference between being relaxed and tense. It simulates discussion about experiences and feelings. It practises the flow of writing.

Cats.

Stimulates bodily awareness, eyes, hands and ear coordination. Laugh and happiness with the cat. Important movements and lines for linking the letter shapes: *a, c, d,* and *g.*

Mandala.

Eye and organisation practice. Stimulates self-awareness, and feelings of responsibility. It increases the security of the basic movements by a shortened repetition of all the different Write Dance themes.

The Write Dance Programme

The Volcano

A combination of stretched and round movements.

A outline for the story.

As you all know a volcano is a very special sort of mountain. Inside, in its stomach, there is an enormous fire. You can never really be certain when the fire is going to burst out - very often it happens suddenly without warning and it surprises both people and animals.

The volcano throws out glowing rocks which are called - that's it - lava. Lava is very fertile if you mix it with soil In order to grow plants of various kinds you also need water, rain for example. In olden times people used to live near volcanoes because the soil was very fertile there. They knew that it could be dangerous, and in spite of that many people still live that way.

Sometimes people too behave a bit like volcanoes. We fill our stomachs with food and drink. When we've eaten too much we get sick, then we don't feel well and suddenly we throw up all our food, often just as unexpectedly as a volcano throws out its great fire, of stones rocks and other contents.

We can also start erupting with words if somebody has teased us for a long time, sometimes you just can't take any more then we want to defend ourselves and maybe that makes us aggressive or if we put up with it, with being teased, we gather a whole load of anger and bad feelings inside us then we get pains in the stomach or the head. We can show our anger with hard words which pour out just like lava and fire does, or as tears. Then maybe the rain comes inside us and tears mean that we at last can relax. When we read, write or draw sometimes it happens that we are very tense.

To learn to be relaxed we are going to practise and play at being volcanoes. First we are going to make body movements to the volcano music and after that you will be able to feel that your body is a lot more relaxed than it was before. Then we are going to make the same movements on big paper with a crayon in each hand.

Sometimes, for one or two children, the volcano with its evocative music can bring out fear and anxiety. This doesn't often happen but be vigilant and keep an eye on how the children are reacting. Let any children who feel like that watch the others so that they can get to grips with the threatening situation and gradually come into the exercise.

Gross Motor Preparation with Music.

The singing and the drums,
Theme 1, is the actual volcano. Swing both arms straight from head height to just below the thighs. Bend your knees in time with the music.

Alternatively you can swing your arms like long distance skiing, or like skiers do.

Choir and drums = eruption.
Throw your arms out parallel in the air, to the right, to the left, forward and backwards, in all directions. You throw out all your tension.

Rhythmic drumming = rocks and the lava falling down.
Shake your whole body, including your head, as fast irregularly and relaxed as you can. Stamp around with your feet.

Thunder and lightening.
Stretch out your arms, high up in the air, as high as you can all along your stretched body, at the same time as everyone breathes deeply in. Hold your breath for a moment and then sink down with your arms rolling around in round movements until you are kneeling. Breathe out slowly, and rest in this position. Repeat that around three times. Listen for the rain which will soon be coming in an irregular movement.

Rain drops.
Practise wrist movements, these are often forgotten. Bend your wrists up in the air up and down at the same speed as the rain. Sometimes perhaps just the fingers.
Vary it a bit, sometimes by just stretching and clenching your fingers. Shut your eyes and stand or hop on one leg while your wrists go up and down, up and down.

Variation - you can have one hand behind your back, the other one high up in the air. You can think of your own variations at the same speed as the rain drops.

Write Dances on movement related pictures.

In Write Dance it matters about movement, not about shape or result. The children can stand or sit, it is the movement that is important. There isn't such a thing as a correct volcano or a growing tree or mandala to try to copy. This is a reason why children find it easy to concentrate on the task.

There isn't anything that's right and nothing is wrong. It's also important that the children have a chance to work with their pictures afterwards and have the chance to complete with more shape oriented details. Children will develop an understanding of the difference between movement focused pictures and form or shape focused pictures.

For Write Dance the height of the table is not important. The children can stand or sit, it is the movement that is important.

Note that the floor is an excellent thing to press a board or paper on. Young children can sit or squat and draw on wallpaper rolls or any other paper rolls and here they get extra good practice in balance, with the upper part of the body.

Stick a big piece of paper on the table with blue tack, at least A3. Take a crayon in each hand, best only to use two colours because more than this gives the children choices which disturb their concentration and flow under the actual exercise, but of course give the children the possibility to work on their pictures afterwards anyway.

Encourage children to use both hands but never force them. It's good if the children can vary between drawing with both hands in parallel and then both hands free or independently and one hand at a time.

Volcano on the paper or a picture with music.

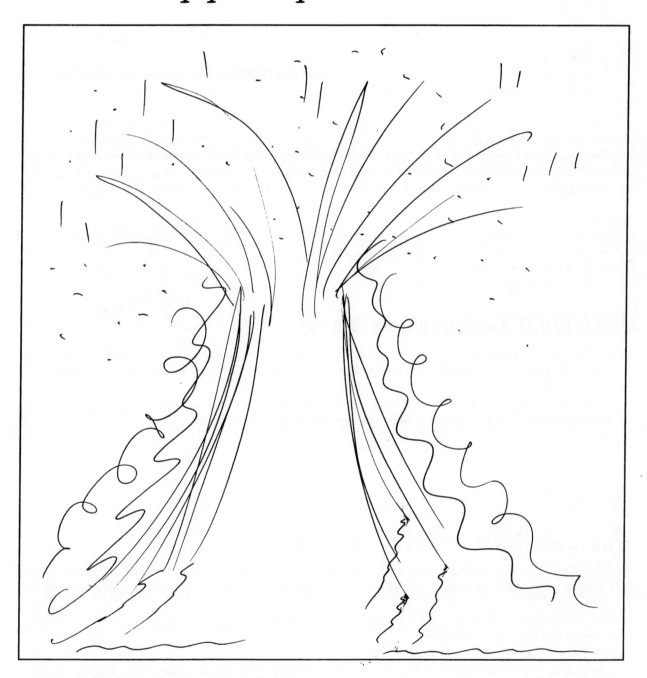

The choir and drums = the actual volcano.

With a crayon in each hand the volcano form is created by swinging the arms up from top to bottom, or from up to down in towards the body at the same speed as the drum, or in time with the drum. Use the help of the whole body, the movements and the lines should be powerful and straight, the crayons built an open triangle which shows the volcano.

Choir and drums again = the eruption.

Out with the stone and the lava, out with the tension and unpleasant feelings. Swing and throw your arms up and outwards in big movements.

Vary by stretching both hands out to the right and then out to the left with the left and right hands working freely in all directions creating the eruption.

African drums.

Make dots of lava or pumice-stone with both hands everywhere on the paper. It's good practice for going out and dividing oneself over a great big empty surface - venturing out. Try later to do this with your hands crossed.

Thunder and Lightening

Breathe in and as you let your breath out make quick round looping movements downwards towards the bottom of the mountain or in slalom motion.

Lava runs downwards.

Raindrops - the rain falls like small dashes which are formed with help from the downward wrist movements. Your hands are like the sort of puppets that are tied on to a string that someone is pulling. Your hands go upwards and downwards at the same time as they make little raindrops when they meet the paper.

Individual Task without Music

Stick a paper on the table with blue tac, draw five volcanoes without music, with one or more chalks or coloured pens, on top of each other. Remember never to try to force children to use both hands.

Let them feel that they want to do that. Use your imagination and work on the picture afterwards, use lots of colours. Compare volcano's drawn with music and without music.

Game on Paper or board in Twos

Stick a paper on the bench or work on the big board and put out four to six chalks or coloured pens. Children will work in twos. Both children should put on a blindfold (see page 20) or shut their eyes.

Use your fingers carefully to feel where the paper's corners or edges of the board are or even better, cover the whole table with paper.

The children should sit beside each other. David, who is sitting on the left, creates the volcano's on the left side, Patrick looks after the right. Let the children work with both hands on their side of the volcano. Decide whether to use music where it's quiet or where the children know the music so well that they can recreate the music and its sound effects together. Four hands and twenty fingers meet, it's a useful social contact as well as an orientation exercise.

Alternative: Katerina starts drawing the volcano with one or more pictures. She keeps one hand on the volcano and with the other she helps Andrew find the picture, here is the volcano and that's where you have to draw lava and stone.

Andrew, who has now drawn the lava and stone for the volcano keeps one hand on the drawing and helps Katerina to orientate herself back to the volcano and says to her "This is where you are going to draw the raindrops". In this case the music shouldn't be used because the children will barely manage to follow it.

The children carry on changing between drawing lava, stones rolling down, raindrops and perhaps water.

Do several volcanoes, you can use the back of the paper. Then it's just that exciting moment when the children can see what they have created together and what the children discover from the proportions and dimensions of the volcano.

Volcano Rhyme

1 - High Volcano shoots out lava
2 - Smoke and Stones fly up and out
3 - Red Sky flaming, stones fall raining!

1 - Swinging arms to the front and backwards while *bending* the knees (bending is important for coordination).

2 - Arms stretching out in the air.

3 - Arms are rolling down in flexible and looped movements.

A Walk in the Country,

... Krongelidong

Round About and Back Again

Free round movements.
A suggested story to explain it.

Last time we talked about the volcano, we threw or shook out of ourselves everything we didn't want in our bodies. Today we are going to collect calm in our bodies, things that make us feel good. The kind of feelings that we get from our imagination, from dreams, these can give us new power, new strength. In order to listen to our good dreams and fantasies we have to sit still and absolutely silent. We are going to let the music help us to relax and find these good thoughts and dreams. If everybody is going to manage this we have to help each other and be absolutely quiet.

Now we are going to turn the sound down (or shut our eyes) and everyone is going to be absolutely silent. While the music is playing we are going to try and imagine a summer landscape (or winter if you prefer, spring or autumn). In our imagination we'll be climbing up a mountain, swimming in a lake or just enjoying the scenery from the top of a mountain. Have a look all around you, you might even find animals or other people. You can even, if you want, go and move in to space, you might find other planets there or space beings, space ships. Talk for a while with the children about what they've seen on their journey when the music finishes. In the beginning let them also hear and imagine things on the reprise which comes after about ten seconds.

When the children understand the music, recognise it and know it well, they can go from listening and just moving quietly to doing the same thing but with chalk, or a crayon in each hand and with their eyes shut, draw the landscape as the music plays on the reprise. Not until the music has finished do they open their eyes and they can then look at their landscapes. Let them work on their pictures and finish them with real pictures of what they have seen along the road, then with the imaginary pictures they are looking for loopy animals - good word for these. Look and find these animals in the lines which are on the paper, change crayons or pens, fill in the lines and do it again and again.

Reinforcing the movements

By letting their hands run along the figures which the children have found again and again they are freed from the fear of doing things wrong because the path is already decided. This means that the experience of the movement, the speed, the power or ease etc. is much more clear. We call this finger dancing.

Uncertainty gives way to certainty and security. This means that the speed can increase and by doing that they find and experience *rhythm* and *elasticity*. After a while try and get them *to experience* that.

Gross Motor Preparations with Music!

For Preschool

Put the lights out, perhaps light a candle to create a mysterious and exciting atmosphere.

Lie on the floor, listen to the music and relax.

Move both arms slowly and softly in the air in time with the music. In the background we hear the raindrops but it is the melody which the children have to recognise to make the curved lines.

Play one minute of the music in the begining, let the children close their eyes or use blindfolds to add variation. You'll find it's enough to have one minute's relaxation because the children aren't used to this situation. (The whole sequence is 2 by 2 minutes).

After a while the children can go and walk around or dance slowly to the music but you need plenty of room to avoid collisions.

For first schools

Let the children sit still at their tables and do the movements sitting down. The children move the top halves of their bodies slowly to the music, neck, arms, wrists, fingers. Some maybe think this is strange but it's often those children who most need relaxation exercises.

Afterwards let the children walk in the country, on paper or the blackboard with music.

Stick a piece of paper on the table and cover your eyes or shut them. Sit quietly and relax but don't be sloppy with posture or concentration. Let the crayon slowly in time with the music wander across all the paper with smooth swelling curved lines and light pressure, watch out for fast or cramped movements. It can be difficult particularly for some boys.

Encourage the children to discover the loopy or typical Write Dance krongelidong animal. Add eyes, a mouth, whiskers, lags and a tail. They can colour it and make special sounds or movements.

With Vangelis melodious "movements" in the background we can hear the last drops of rain from the volcano exercise. Let the children try to get in to an imaginary world, like silence after the storm.

Sometimes lively but insecure children can have difficulty with this exercise. They often press too hard and go too quickly over the writing surface. Try letting these children use the wrong hand try also to let them hold the crayons or chalk between the thumb and first finger or place from above between their bent first and middle fingers.

Inspire them by yourself drawing a loopy animal (krongelidong) on the board, that can often help. While they are drawing and imagining the music can carry on playing in the background.

Paper games in twos

A - Stick the paper on the table - we are doing orientation in a wood. Draw 3 - 5 dots distributed over the whole paper. Look carefully where they are and try to remember them.

Alex holds the help hand (equals the non writing hand) on a dot while Jane puts the blindfold on him, or encourages him to shut his eyes. Alex starts with a pen slowly circling around the first dot - the check point, then he continues with the crayon to another dot and tries to circle around that - does he remember where it is? Jane can perhaps help by leading him (orally) upwards towards the dot. Carry on in this way. Open eyes, how many dots has Alex managed to find and circle round. Maybe he's run around like a hunting dog in all directions. Do the children see any shapes or figures in the orienteering. Fill them in another colour.

Finish them off with eyes and ears or a tail. Here is another krondelidong animal.

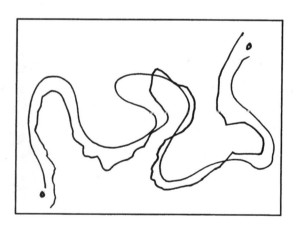

B - Let Marlene draw a winding road in the form of parallel lines. Just like above she can help Alexby putting his help first finger on the road and letting him find his way.

C - Make free loopy animals on big paper and reinforce them by repeating the movement with different clours. Cut out the loopy animals and stick them up on big bits of paper or on the wall.

D - Stick a sheet of paper on the table.
Charlie draws five different things e.g. a tree, house or aeroplane, a gnome, an animal.
Charlie gives a crayon or pen to Marlene who shuts her eyes or uses a blindfold. He leads her to a starting point, where ever he wants.

After that Charlie leads the first finger of her assisted hand to one of the figures on the paper. This demands a little bit more finger and hand acrobatics which also gives them some practice in social contact and makes the exercise a little bit more exciting.

When Charlie has put Marlene's finger in a new place, he encourages her: "Now you are going to fly or cycle or hop like a bird, climb, ski, slalom from here to your little finger". This carries on until Marlene, after several different means of transport, is back at the starting point again.
Both children practise with open eyes before the game starts and then Charlie and Marlene change roles.

flying or aeroplane tracks in the sky   **climbing**

bird tracks   **slalom tracks**

swinging your way forward   **hopping.**

Krongelidong rhyme

1 - Slithery, Sliding, Slime
2 - Twisting turning rhyme
3 - Think of an animal with spots or stripes
4 - Give it two eyes but don't get a fright
5 - Your creature is friendly and coloured so bright.

1 Twist your whole body in winding movements. Don't forget to bend the neck and the wrists in an excessive way.
2 Stand still. One child may imagine an animal, i.e. a giraffe, an elephant, a mouse...
3 Winding movements again
4. Another child imagines a nonsense or sound word of the animal. For example: giraffe - pliafe, elephant - snabant, mouse - plouse. It should not exist because after that we make its movements, its sound and draw it on board or on paper.

An exercise on the big blackboard

One child stands in front of the blackboard. All the children together say the rhyme and do the movements. The child at the board draws and makes concrete the slithering movements with the chalk at the same time as the assisted hand, with similarly slithering movements. After the rhyme the child at the blackboard puts on a blindfold and draws the rhyme figure which the group have decided. The children then take turns to create the figures on the board.

Remember that krongelidong animals;
- should be made of one single line, ideally with the same start and end point
- should be drawn with round, soft and calm moves
- even tense shapes are also interesting to discover or invent.

Through this playful exercise the children are practising future letters and links.

To do something at the blackboard in front of a whole group can be quite frightening for some but challenging for others. The game helps to take away the fear of failure, the more happy and imagination filled the better. Laughing together helps us to develop.

Are children ready for the next theme?
If not, perhaps go over this one again or go back to the volcano.

Circles and Eights

round movements.

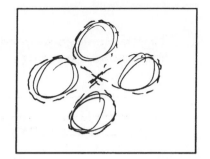

In our alphabet the letters and figures are made of straight and curved lines, (demonstrate straight and curved letters and figures in the air and on the blackboard: A - 3 - I - 8 etc.).

a 3 8 S   i b d g g

To join up the letters we need to do round or at least rounded pen movements, that makes your handwriting move faster and it's better and easier than if we write sharply with lots of edges and corners. Some adults link their letters just with sharp corners, like this:

We must always try and do curves where there should be curves and straight where it should be straight. A round ball rolls itself but a square cube hops just for one turn.

A dice has to have rounded corners if it's going to roll well. The steps that you climb up have to be straight not curved. Can you think of some other examples? If we don't learn round movements letters will look like this (that's the one in the third load of drawings with the two figures in the middle).

They are called crows feet. This is how they should look:

E g a t t

Printed letters, big ones just like little, are all the same height and width. They are like a row of nice stable trees along a road. With a computer you can move letters up and down, to the left and to the right by pressing on a key, but they don't fall over, they always stand straight up.

W R I T I N G   w r i t i n g

Hand written letters on the other hand, are different from each other. They live and move, they vary a little from one time to the next, they vary a lot from person to person.

Written letters are like human bodies, even when we are sitting still there is life and movement in the brain, the heart, the lungs and nerves. Letters live as well, you can say that they live with each other. Show on the board.

The children will gradually begin to understand the link between the body and letters. The letters have almost become living beings.

When we write we move the pen all the time, up and down, left, right, horizontally and vertically. The figure of a four leafed clover which we are going to do this week gives us good practice in the different directions. The teacher can demonstrate this on the blackboard.

Lying, sleeping, resting eight.

Standing eight is the cat, at eight it is standing up!

The combination gives the four leafed clover.

The brains, the bodies, the arms and the fingers movements all hang together and that's why it's good to practise round eights with the body first. Learning to skip can be hard in the beginning but after a bit of practice you can do it without thinking, it happens automatically. It's the same thing with practising writing, first we practise the movements in the air and on the paper and after a while we are sure of the different letter shapes.

Gross Motor Preparation with Music

The children stand behind the tables, in a ring on the floor or they spread out into the room if it's a gym/play hall.

Let the music lead the arms in big slow circles outwards and inwards.

Bend the knees in time with the music, try shutting your eyes sometimes.

The music changes to a slower tempo.

With your hands together make eights in the air, both lying and standing, sleeping and awake.

Stretch your arms out properly to the right and to the left.

Let shoulders and thighs join in.

Shut your eyes when you can feel that it's going well.

Circles and eights on paper or blackboard with music

Fold a rectangular piece of paper in half, stick it onto the table with blue tac then draw a dot on the left hand in the middle of the left half and a dot in the right hand on the right hand half. This is good eye and balance practice. Put the music on and move your arms calmly and softly in big circles outwards and inwards. When the music stops the children get a crayon in each hand and make two big circles around the dots, inwards and outwards.

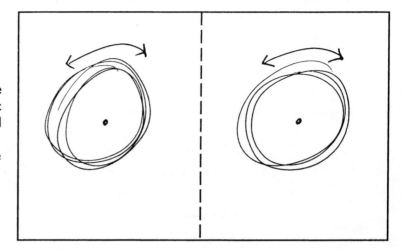

Variations

Vary, if you like, by letting the circles around the dots in the middle grow or shrink.

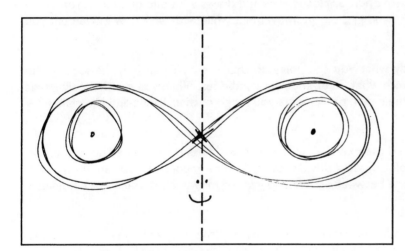

Lying eights

Put a little cross halfway in between the two central dots (on the fold). This is the starting point for the lying down eights' movement, this is where the lines should cross.

With a crayon in the writing hand or in both hands with your hands tied together a big eight is now drawn with a light pressure round the circles which have already been created.

Place the eights a little bit outside the circles - see the example - shut your eyes and draw when it feels as though things are going well, when it feel good.

Change direction, many children do have problems with crossing their own lines which shows very clearly in this theme. It is not at all uncommon to see figures like this.

 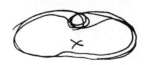 

This has to do with the very complex cooperation between the eye and brain signals and cortex. The cooperation between the two halves of the brain, between the eyes and between the left and right body halves does not develop equally quickly. With the eight-exercise, children learn to dare "crossing-over" and to discover the other half.

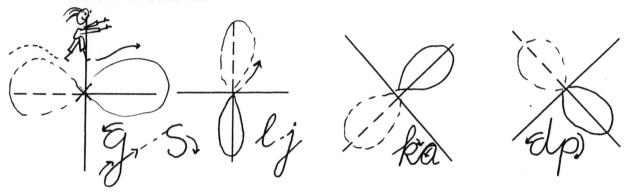

Children who find it hard to cross over the line

The child stands or sits at the table with open or closed eyes and draws with one or two crayons. Very softly and slowly you nudge the child's hand in the eight movement while with each new movement you say "Cross over".

Speak clearly each time about exactly what you are doing so that the child can join the idea of the movement direction and the feeling with what he or she hears and does. When you get the feeling that the child is in control or controlling their own movements you let go of their hands and the child now continues, perhaps with their eyes shut.

Children often react very positively to these exercises as if a new world has been opened up to them. In a way it has, from the motor skills point of view this discovery is very important. You can always help children in this way e.g. trying to change between arcade and garland movements which can be difficult in the beginning.

The movement should be soft and round. Make sure that the pressure isn't too hard. The music leads the children towards the slow movements and helps them get in touch with their inner feelings. This can be irritating for some children who prefer to work quickly and with sharp hard movements.

When children have mastered the lying or sleeping eights' movements, shape and distribution, they can carry on without music, use a crayon or perhaps an object e.g. a little car to follow the shape. Repeat the movements and create their own sounds for each one.

This can be used as a way of discharging energy for certain children. Vary if you wish, between slow movement with music and fast without music so you can experience the difference.

Individual exercises without Music

Do circles and eights just like before but now without music.
Use your imagination and create for example, owl, eyes, glasses, a butterfly but note that the corners must be rounded.

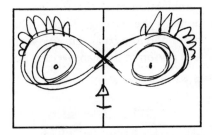 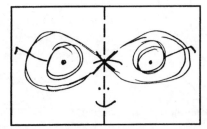 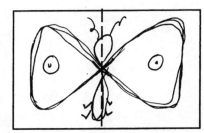

Clover-eight

Fold the paper into four bits, mark a circle in the middle of each fold line (four). The exercise gives practice and feelings for proportions and divisions.

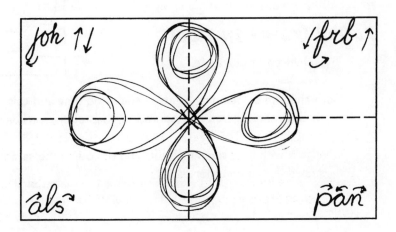

Continue the exercise with lying eights and standing eights, link them up to a four leafed clover. Try and get soft changes of direction, listen, the music will lead you.

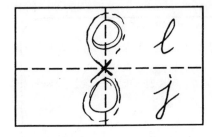 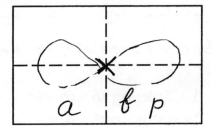 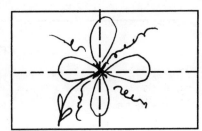

After a while try different ways of joining up the four leafed clover. Sometimes in the opposite direction, anticlockwise and sometimes clockwise.

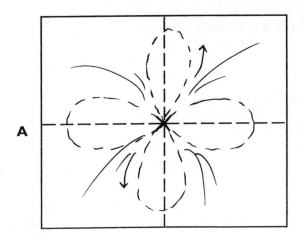 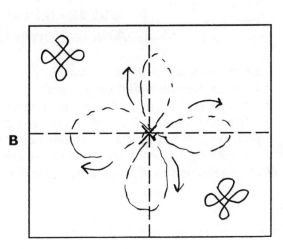

In Write Dance two we develop these movements further, they are very important for general balance. The clover eight can also be executed abstractly in the air but it is harder in fact than on paper because these more complicated movements are more difficult to take an over-view of and to control. It is easy to lose your direction but children learn a lot faster than we believe, very often. Use several colours when repeating in the movements, make big and small flowers by adding stalks with soft lines, light lines coming out from the clover flower.

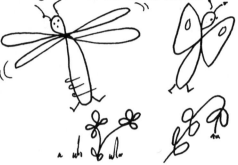

The clover eight is a combination of all the changes of direction which are found in the writing process. The more the brain is programmed in a balanced way with this movement, the more rhythmic the handwriting is.

Paper Game in twos

Two children sit at a table.

Both children do standing eights at the same time and this means that a clover eight develops through the children's co-operation, adaptation, consideration and co-ordination.

Change it with lying/sleeping eights and of course the same result is achieved. Cut them out, stick them up on other paper.

The circle and eights rhyme

1 - Spining in - in - in
2 - Spining - out - out - out
3 - Circle up - and circle down
4 - Turning left and turning right
5 - The lazy eight sleeps with me at night
6 - But at eight o'clock we do wake up
7 - And we jump then as a clickety cup.

1 Circle movements with arms inwards
2 Circle movements with arms outwards
3 Circle movements on your chest and on your stomach
4 Circle movements with the left hand alternatively with right hand
5 With joined hands we make a sleeping eight in front of us
6 Standing eight over the chest and on the stomach
7 Imagine some sort of funny jumping movements

Robot

Straight movement

Proposal for an introductory talk.

Angles, triangles and quadrilaterals are needed for big letters and figures but also for little ones,

HLde... HLde...

sharp   rounded.

We also need straight lines for other things e.g. when we underline or when we have got to divide a piece of paper, but also in the letter itself.

Rounded lines are needed when we join letters together.

Straight and round are opposites, rounded-off is in-between; just like a bridge between tense and relaxed, breathing in breathing out, hard and soft, slow and fast. We need a change in our daily life and so does handwriting.

The opposites in a dance can create a rhythm. There are many different rhythms in life, the birds that fly in a flock have each got their own way of flying but together it makes up a rhythm. Singers in a choir have got different voices, different pitches and rhythms but together it makes one unity, one rhythm. Waves in the sea are created of different heights, different lengths, different depths but together it makes one rhythm.

Can you think of any more examples?

Can you name some big letters,
- *capital letters that are formed from a straight line? H, K, L, E, F and T.*
- *some big letters that are formed from round lines or curved lines, S, C and O,*
- *some big letters that are built of straight and round lines are B and D.*
- *some figures that are built just of straight lines are 1, 4 and 7. Some that are round are 0, 3 and 8.*

Both round and straight are 2, 5, 6 and 9. Almost all lower case letters are built up of both straight and round shapes.

O→O ||↕→| a→a b→b→ab

Along with the music in this section it's easy to count slowly 1 2 1 2,
or twice as fast 1 2 3 4 - 1 2 3 4.

We call that the beat. The tones together make a melody. The clock's ticking is a beat. It's hard to count in tune but we can sing tunes and stamp out the beat with our feet. In Frere Jaques both beat and tone are sung together. Sing it in the group, one group sings the melody with its text and the other emphasises the rhythm with ding dong during the whole song.

Now we will start with our feet left right, left right while we count 1 2, 1 2, or 1 2 3 4, 1 2 3 4. How would a robot do it? Let some children show it. Let's practise Write Dance's robot movements without music and then we'll do it in time with the music or with our own sounds.

Gross Motor preparation with Music

Let the children stand in a circle opposite each other or walking around in the room/gym hall/play hall. Follow the beat of the music, bend and stretch the arms from the shoulders up down up down, in out in out. Let this happen in straight definite movements.

Change between the different beats and say at the same time 1 2 1 2 slowly and 1 2 3 4 1 2 3 4 faster, change around.

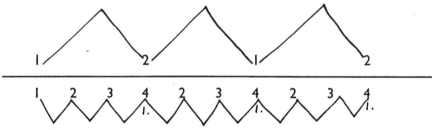

Easier variation;

Let the children move around freely in the hall like robots. They will get completely caught up in the game and they may forget to listen to the beat, don't correct them. Musical children will probably follow the beat but the others will gradually learn.

Robot on the paper with Music

Bend a piece of paper, in the middle and stick it on the table. In the middle of each half the children should make a dot which is good practice for hand eye coordination. Together and preferably with both hands do several straight lines with squares on top of each other round the dots, clockwise or anticlockwise in different directions with the hands.

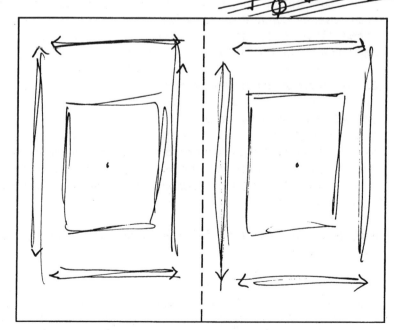

Variation.

At first just do up and down lines then change colour and do horizontal lines over them, this will create a grid or do it diagonally.

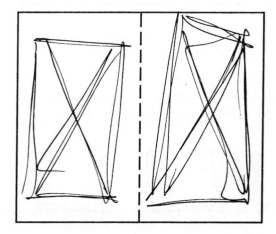 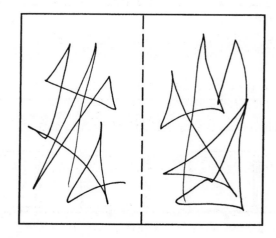

The resulting movements are firm, straight and pointed straight lines.

Individual Practice Without Music

Draw mountain tops at the same time as you are talking to yourself. Say to yourself 1 2 1 2 1 2.

It is important for the children to get used to saying out loud what they are doing. When children learn to read they also learn to read out loud. This is important for the programming of the brain. For learning to read the brain needs to hear what it sees and in learning to write the brain needs to hear what the hand does. Help and encourage children who feel shy about this, let them practise in smaller groups at first.

Variation

Fold piece of paper in four. Fold first the middle part and then fold it over once more. Folding is an important exercise for hand eye coordination and also for practising the ability to concentrate. Draw five squares evenly distributed on each of the three fold lines. In order to distribute five structure shapes (as they are called in Write Dance), along a row you have to do the following: put the assisting hand's first finger exactly even with the left edge of the paper. Put a dot just to the right of the finger and then do the same on the right.

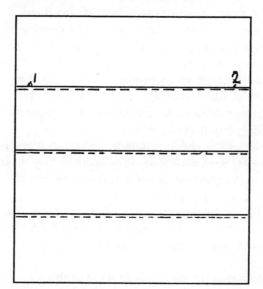

Place dot 3 half way between the two marks.

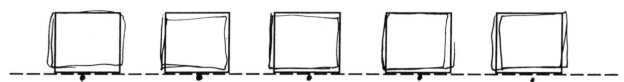

Place dot 4 between 1 and 3 and dot 5 between 3 and 2.

Then draw the squares just above the dots.

Follow the cubes with another crayon. Each change of direction has to be a clear square, this could be a knight's castle. Change colour, repeat the movement 2 or 3 times on top of each other, add some soldiers if you want. Don't use any structure shapes in the bottom row.

Draw the Knight's castle with the help of your voice, count 1 2 3 4 etc. Use your imagination to develop and work on these shapes, perhaps they are houses in an old town, let the ground be covered in stones in the form of small definite lines. This gives the children practice at looking and dividing things over a whole surface, a way of preparing them to divide up words across the surface. This pattern can also be a frame and a decoration around pictures or written exercises.

Game on paper in twos.

Give out copies of the 'ruler distance ruled' paper. That means paper ruled with roughly the width of a ruler - can be copied from page 22.

Let the children sit opposite each other, they can be either A or B.
Both children have their own crayons in different colours,
Both children start on the same edge but on each side of the line and they make ⋀⋁⋁⋀ or walls at the same time.

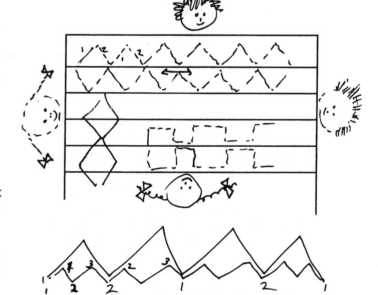

This can be done slowly while they count aloud 1 2 1 2 or at double speed 1 2 3 4 1 2 3 4 when they are more confident.

Note that the pens should meet at the same time at the line.

The purpose is that the children can work together, cooperate, and experience the same speed. It is a very suitable exercise for a child and adult to do together.

Robot Rhyme

1 - Metal clinking and clanking a lot
2 - No w I move just like a robot.
3 - All my fingers stretching out
4 - It's time to turn and look about.

1 Arms stretch out in the air (bend the knees if possible)
2 Down on the shoulders (stretching the knees again)
3 Arms stretch out to the left and right
4 Back to the shoulders
5 Repeat these movements
7 Make a turn on the spot

Make sure that the knees are bending, remind the children now and then: bend your knees to get nice underloops.

This is where we have the descenders, assuming children know about the letters' lower, middle and underparts (see p.15).

Are the children ready to go further?
If not, repeat the earlier theme first.

The Train

Arcades, garlands and loops -

Proposal for the introductory story.

The teacher may ask "do you remember what we have been practising for the last four weeks? First the volcano with the big movements on the paper, then..." Let the children try to remember and also what the purpose was.

Now we are going to practise the loops and we are going to train our fingers in quick movements. Our fingers are going to learn to work like tiny little puppets with their bending and stretching muscles.

The more we practise this play with our fingers the better and easier it will be to draw and write later. In the week theme we are going to play and talk about trains with their great big wheels connected by a rod which goes round, round, up and down.

(Demonstrate with both arms and explain again the words garlands and arcade.)

The engine driver pulls on the whistle: "Beep Beep now we are rolling". Now we are going to play trains with just our arms, close to your chests and thighs we roll along. At the same time we are going to sound like an engine - "choo choo", first slowly and then faster and faster. The whistle blows and we stretch our arms high up.

Variation

With the wrists we make two trains which are going away from and towards each other. With outstretched rolling wrists we push them out to the side and in towards the middle again and automatically they become garlands with the loops upwards in one direction and arcades with the loops downwards in the other.

Demonstrate this on the board and explain the concepts and what they mean.

Garlands

Arcades.

If we take away the hanging down loops you still have the arcade, bow and the arches. Demonstrate on the board, mark with coloured chalk the top parts of the arches.

If we take away the upward pointing loops the garland, bowl or boat is still there. Demonstrate this by using a sponge on the blackboard.

We have practised circles in theme 3,

Arcades are created in this way,

a circle movement starting to the right is stretched out.

Garlands are created like this,

a circle movements starting to the left is widening out.

Five to six year olds can find the change of direction difficult in the beginning. If that is the case let the child with the pen or chalk go round in circles to left or right for a while. Maybe nudge their arm carefully towards the right. The child will discover the arcade or garland movement.

Two joined e-letters are made of looped garland movements. Show this on the blackboard and sound at the same time, like a steam engine "choo choo". If we stretch out the 'e' shape then it leads to a looped 'l' shape.

Variation

choo choo   choo choo   choo choo choo choo

The combination of *b* and *h*, they are all arcade and garland links.   *b h*

The resemblance to a train and the music helps children to make their movements quickly and rhythmically without thinking about how they are going to be joined together.

This is a restraint movement whilst loops feel much more natural to write. Handwriting will therefore flow more smoothly.

Breathing Exercises

Now we are going to do the train sound very very slowly through our noses and mouths. We do this to practise breathing and to train our lungs.

When we breathe in the right way, we are relaxed and that makes it much easier to think, read, count and write. With our mouths closed, we are going to breathe in slowly through our noses and with a "pooh" sound we are going to breathe out through our mouths.

We do this five times. Count on your fingers.

It's going to be very slow in the beginning because the train is heavy and the passengers mustn't fall over when it leaves the station.

We are going to do this least five times but then we are going to use our arms for help. When we breathe in we lift our hands up, when we breathe out we let them down again in looped circle movements.

Be careful not to make your neck or shoulders tense. Do the exercise sitting down or go round in a circle very slowly.

Let the children create flowers at the same time as they audibly breathe in, and blow out. The petals can be drawn to the right or the left. The pen's movement should follow the same beats, if possible.

This is a good practice for shape awareness, concentration and body coordination.
Use the sponges on the blackboards to make lines.

Gross Motor Preparation with Music

Do the same exercises as in the introductory story. Let the wrists roll along as well. Carry straight on with the train on the paper or blackboard with music.

Materials

A big piece of paper and two crayons per child are needed.

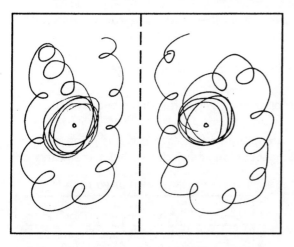

Fold the paper in the middle along the long side and stick it on the table. Let the children, who are now used to this put a dot in the middle of each side, very good for eye training. When the music is playing the children circle around the middle mark with both hands, one chalk in each hand, to the left or the right.

After that the journey carries on along the circle trail around the edges of the paper, both hands work together (lateralisation). Put a mark in each corner which will serve as a station where the crayon can stop and go round in circles; maybe the passengers get off or on here. Make sure that the circle movements are soft and relatively quick.

The train's motor (the writing hand) should be moving all the time. Begin the train journey along the edges of the paper but then carry on with a diagonal cross with looped garland and arcade movements. Let the train make a new track and also go along the same one.

This is a good overview for training for the surface and the edges/margins. Use a lot of different colours, don't let the circles get too big. About an inch is right, 2 - 3 cm.

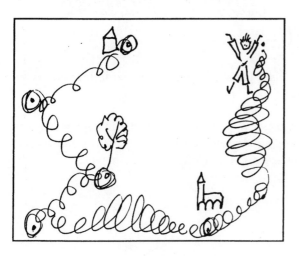

Variation

Free movement over the paper - like a Walk in the country.

Play music and pause it now and again. Let the children find a place whilst they are circling around the station. This is good for coordination of thought and writing. Then we can carry on to Granny, in Scotland, cousins in Cornwall, etc.

Make use of the music volume: high for big loops and low for little.

Train without Music

Fold an A4 piece of paper in to four parts. Let the children draw lines along the folds, don't use a ruler. Learning to do a straight line towards the right is a very important hand- eye coordination exercise.

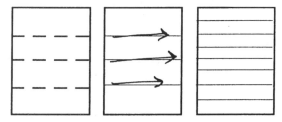

Draw another seven lines between those that are there which makes rows, again without a ruler. Let those who think it is difficult turn the paper through a quarter turn and draw the lines downwards towards themselves. This will become a routine in Write Dance part 2.

Mark the stations by drawing a dot far on the left and then to the right, either on or between, the rails.

The train is going to drive from the left to the right station, the dot. At each dot it is going to circle around a few times, then continue straight down to the next station and circles, round it, then carry on towards the left.

We call this 'plough wise' because that is how farmers plough their fields. In this way the loops swap almost automatically between arcade and garland movements.

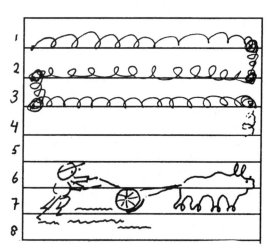

The Greeks originally wrote in this way, left right, right left. In Egypt you see hieroglyphics drawn both towards the left and towards the right. It is said that man is talking to God towards the right but God talks to men towards the left.

In France there is a proverb "Man writes on the lines, God writes between the lines". The plough method proves to be an attractive means of changing the direction of the loops and thereby the eye brain signals in a natural way.

Mirror writing, which is quite common in children under six and which can still be natural for some adults, is perhaps not just a signal disturbance but something that has a deep psychological basis.

Use several colours on top of each other.
The loops should ideally not go into each other like this...

but like this......

This practises letter distance, between letters and organisation.

Turn the paper a quarter turn so that it is lying down, and let the children form the loops towards and away from themselves: a "Chinese plough" shape.

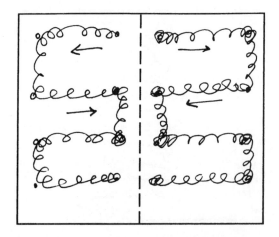

Variation 1
Fold a big piece of paper in the middle and stick it to the table. Plough with one crayon in each hand in towards the fold, down out towards the edges or with both hands in the same direction, towards the right straight down, towards the left.

Variation 2
First draw a load of square or rectangular railway trucks above the line or the fold, then draw the rolling wheels, let them have four wheels in an arcade or with a garland movement, count aloud. Carry on making these wheels to music.

Develop it and work on it afterwards to make the train look nice.

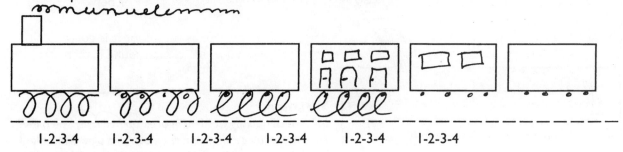

1-2-3-4   1-2-3-4   1-2-3-4   1-2-3-4   1-2-3-4   1-2-3-4

The Train Game in Twos

Sit opposite each other one by one. Each pair needs a piece of A4 paper with a ruler distance lines or folds.

Two children begin at the same time and play and make arcades or garlands.

  a Their pens meet at the line or the fold
  b Count the loops together 1 2 3 4 5, or make train noises at the pen meeting point (choo choo).

Listen carefully to each other in order to coordinate movements.

Variation.
The Journey Game is done in the same way as the game on paper - page 37. Demonstrate different modes of travel at the blackboard.

flying ⟵―――――――――――⟶ fast

train (arcades or garlands) ～～～～～ medium fast

the robot, ⌐_⌐_⌐_⌐_ slow

Use your voice to help. *metal clinking* ......⋅ᴵᶠ See more examples on page 37.

Caroline shuts her eyes or uses a blindfold and holds a pen in her writing hand. At the same time Ariane draws five figures (the paper is stuck down to the table)

Ariane places Caroline's writing hand on one of the figures and her assistant hand/help hand index finger on the next figure.

Ariane decides the method of travel between the different figures.

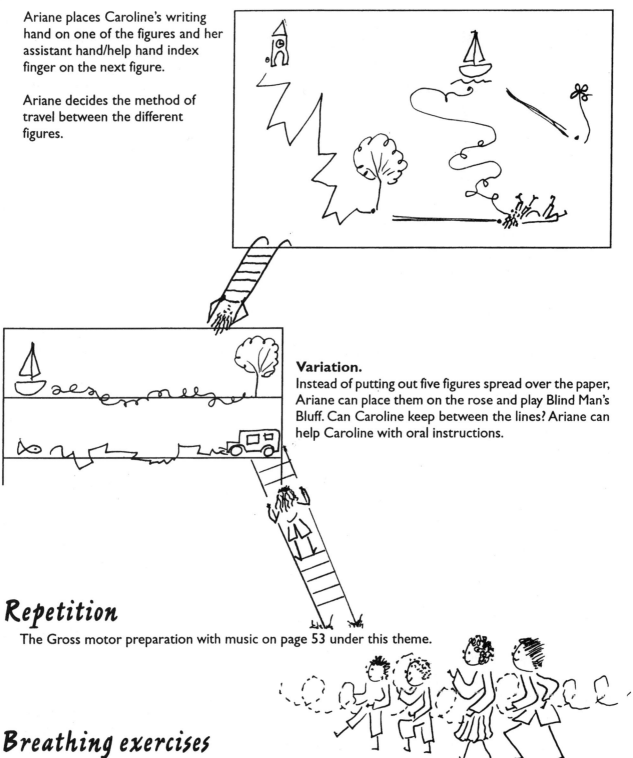

Variation.
Instead of putting out five figures spread over the paper, Ariane can place them on the rose and play Blind Man's Bluff. Can Caroline keep between the lines? Ariane can help Caroline with oral instructions.

Repetition
The Gross motor preparation with music on page **53** under this theme.

Breathing exercises

Intersperse these things now and again with breathing exercises.

With mouths closed everybody breathes in quietly through their noses and with an audible "pooh" and breathes out through their mouths.

Do this in a calm rhythm five times, you can count on your fingers if you want. Move your arms like the wheels of a locomotive, with your elbows bent, which turn forward and backward but held in close to the body.

The Growing Tree

A combination of straight lines and round movements.

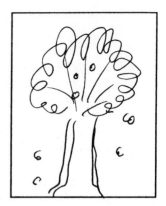

<u>Proposal for an introductory story.</u>

A little seed falls down to the ground. An acorn and a beech seed look different. The trees appearance, size, colour and leaves are already predetermined in the tiny seed.

If there is a lot of rain in the autumn or winter the seed is washed away and never grows up to be a big tree; it just disappears. It can also happen that there is too much sun, like in Spain or Zambia, and then the seed dries out. If the seed falls in the right place at the right time and gets just the right amount of water and heat, it will grow and get bigger, but even then the danger isn't over. You can still have too much rain, wind or sun. An animal might eat up the small plants or a person's foot can also tread on it.

Out of the hundred million seeds from a tree maybe only eight or ten actually germinate and grow up. We can compare plants and trees with letters. Handwritten letters live in their own special way. A person's handwriting develops and grows and ends up looking like a special style. Some of them we can see very clearly but others disappear almost in the movements of the handwriting.

Typewritten letters, on the other hand, are made of a fixed shape. They are always printed in the same size and with the same pressure, they don't live or move. They are like bricks in a wall. Letters stand for a sound, the way we should form our mouths, tongue and lips. Since we are all so different we speak differently as well, some slow, gentle and soft. Others have a sharp tone in their voice. Our voices are a part of our personality.

When we write we do the same. We all create our own letters and numbers in our own way. Some people press hard with the pen, others more carefully, some write big, others small, some write with round shapes and others with sharp ones.

These are as many ways of writing as there are people. Our handwriting, our way of forming letters and linking them together is as unique as our finger prints.
Also the letters and numbers are different from time to time or from one time to another. Sometimes you look at them and you think 'that looks nice' but at other times they are ugly or illegible. Sometimes it feels so easy, but other times it is such hard work to write and to draw. Our way of forming letters is linked to body movements, how our fingers, wrists and arms function and can move.

We practise that sort of thing all the time in Write Dance but there is also something that influences our handwriting which we can't see. What is it?
(Let the children suggest).

It is our brain activity, we call it signals or reflexes. Also our lungs, feelings and nerves are on the go or moving. Sometimes they are visible, people can shake from fear, or shudder from something unpleasant. We can jump or dance with joy, pant from exertion, but sometimes you can't see it, your heart can beat faster because of extra tension and excitement. You can get butterflies in your stomach from excitement (Ask for more examples.)

*We all have our own way of being. Everything which lives has its own rhythm. When you hear music you hear melodies and rhythm, you dance to the rhythm of the music. When you listen to the sea you are listening to the rhythm of the sea which is the sea's life. When you see a flock of birds flying along, again you can see rhythm, each bird flies in its own way but at a distance they have a common rhythm. In order to be able to write letters that have life and rhythm we have to first practise, train our ears **to hear** the rhythms, our eyes **to see** the rhythms and our bodies **to feel** them. With this music we are going to let a tree grow with everything that's on it, the trunk, branches and leaves, we are going to practise the movements first. They are almost the same as the volcano. First we are going to plant the trunk, put it down with straight arms outstretched in front of the body, we swing them downwards outside our thighs and knees and bend the knees. Then we put in four branches in all directions and throw the arms out in all directions. It is now time to put leaves on the trees and the wrists roll round the imaginary branches. Finally we are going to pick berries and fruit from the branches. Stretch your arms out in all directions and reach for berries, some have perhaps fallen down to the ground.*

Gross Motor Preparations with Music

Children stand behind the table in a ring on the floor or they spread themselves round the room or play hall. First we are going to practise the movements without music. Straight and round movements are very similar to the volcano movements but you have to count aloud in order to follow the beats of the music.

The Growing Tree consists of four themes: the trunk, the branches, the leaves and the apple theme. Since the first downward movements come right at the very beginning you can prepare the children with a running race - "ready, steady, go"! This increases the attention/excitement and also the concentration.

Count out loud for all the movements. Do movements first without music.

The Trunk Theme - swing the arms power-fully downwards, twice and bend your knees.

The Branch Theme - swing the arms powerfully up-wards in different directions four times.

The Trunk and Branch theme are repeated.

The Leaf Theme is round hand movements, leaves are formed on the branches. The branch and leaf theme repeated.

The Apple Theme, with both hands we will pick ap-ples with gripping movements. We have to stretch out high in the air, low down towards the ground and in all directions.

The Leaf and Apple theme repeated twice after which the music stops.

The music comes back after ten seconds. Repeat the exercise and continue the work on paper, or on a blackboard.

The Growing Tree on paper or blackboard with Music.

Stick a big piece of paper on the table. Start by being in body and soul like growing trees, as was described earlier. The imaginary drawing movements are like the volcano's. The movements and illustrations are described on the previous page.

The Apple Theme where we pick berries or fruit, is illustrated with intensive circular movements.

You can vary it a bit with some flying birds illustrated with quick 'V' shapes.

The movements are a combination of swinging and stretching or straight lines, arcades and garland movements. Listen consciously to the music, it helps and this will lead you into the movement. If this is too difficult for some children then let them, in the beginning, choose their own movements for the music.

Do use all the paper. The more colourful formed the tree is the happier and more balanced the child is likely to be.

If you want you can repeat the exercise on the other side of the paper with a blindfold or shutting the eyes; then feel and look at the difference!

Give the children time to do further work on the tree with their own imagination, perhaps with birds' nests, sun, clouds, animals, plants on the ground.

Growing Tree without Music

Let the children decide whether they want to work alone or together.

Here it is a question of working with both hands and drawing a forest of growing trees, with or without blindfolds. If the children use both hands encourage them to feel the difference between the writing hand and the help hand. They will definitely notice the difference, they will be able to experience it.

The help hand is much less developed, practised, trained. Never force a child to use both hands.

The idea is that it should feel fun and exiting. Compare the movements with and without the music. Can you see a difference?

Talk about it.

Variation

For two children. Oscar draws a tree with his trunk and branches in the writing dance way. Suzanna creates spring with leaves. This exercise can also be done as blind man's buff.

The Growing Tree Rhyme.

1 - A seed in the ground
1 - By no-one, I was found
2 - Toes are wobbling, roots are hobbing
3 - I grow up
4 - I grow out
5 - I grow high
6 - The sun makes me stronger
6 - Branches grow longer
7 - Red, green and brown
7/8 - Fruit are falling down

1 Squat down on the flloor, the fingertips in front of you as a support.
2 Lift your feet several times, but with the hands still on the floor as support
3 Start stretching the legs
4 Strech the knees, the legs almost straight
5 Stretch out as high as you can
6 - Round wrist movements
7 Round wrist movements with the arms sunk down
7/8 We sink down on to the floor and repeat the rhyme

And so it starts again, as many times as seems useful.
Start slowly and gradually increase the tempo on the
second and third time.

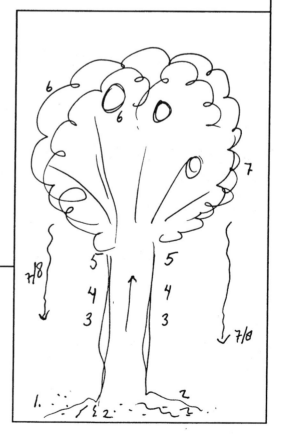

Variation
Draw the tree with both hands along to the rhyme

60

Silver Wings over the Sea

Flowing up and down movements

The music which is played is called Silver Wings.

You can tell the story of Jonathan the Seagull. He was a seagull who left the group to explore the world. While he was out alone he developed a lot and when he came back he found it difficult to be accepted again. Richard Bach's "Jonathan Livingstone's Seagull" is a fascinating book.

During this writing dance section there are good opportunities relating to sea and water. The atmosphere gradually becomes like it was in the Walk in the country, quiet and relaxed. The children can rest their heads on a table, sit in a ring or lie on the floor while the music is playing.

Let them make slow swinging movements with their whole body and with swaying wave-making hands in front of them, or let them just listen and enjoy the piece. Encourage the children to use their imaginations and look at inner pictures or give them an imaginary situation:

For example:

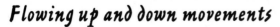

"You are sitting alone in a boat, the sun is warm and you feel calm and happy. Far far away on the horizon something is coming slowly towards you.

   What is it?
   Another boat?

Or do you perhaps see an island or maybe a seal or a whale.
Maybe you are a bird with silver wings, a seagull flying over land and sea.

   What do you see?
   What do you feel?"

Gross Motor Preparations with Music

Children sit or lie in a ring on the floor in a circle.
Turn the lights down, shut the eyes, put the music on and let the children move freely to the music.
Encourage the children to listen intensively to the music and feel how it helps them to move in swinging movements and rhythm.
Let their hands swing around in wave movements.
Try to get the same atmosphere as with the Walk in the country.

Silver wings on paper or blackboard with music.

Stick a big bit of paper on the table, preferably a soft one that easily sucks up water e.g. water colour paper or wall paper. Brushes, water, green and blue finger paints are needed. Damp the paper first with a sponge.

Let the children experience how beautiful it feels to make slow soft wave movements along to the music, to mix the colours and create the sea. Encourage them to shut their eyes.

Crayons can be used as well but with water colours you get more of a sea experience. When the music has finished the children can work on their pictures and finish them off with seagull wings, fish and boats.

This develops the overview and the ability of looking and being able to divide oneself over large surfaces. It may also arouse a feeling of freedom. Keep an eye on and help the children who can't manage the up and down movements, they will probably soon end up with pure arcade, or garland movements....

instead of the wave.

These difficulties are not uncommon in the beginning. Even some adults find it hard to create these waves with soft and rhythmic lines. Up and down movements are a combination of arcade and garland movements in one continuous movement. It is just that this makes it difficult in the beginning.

The changing nature of the movements are difficult for the brain to register and programme itself to do. Here you can help the child in the same way as with the eight movements. Stand behind or beside the child and lead their hands by the wrists until the brain has programmed in the up and down movement. Use the support form (see more under structure, wave, movement page 64).

Movements - Soft slow swaying movements with very light free wave movements up and down. They will probably look like long stretched out snakes.

The Distribution - It is important that the whole paper is used, the children can decide themselves how much is going to be sea and how much is going to be sky. Preferably the whole paper should be full of waves. Be prepared for the fact that some children find it hard to leave the nice safe edges.

Individual practice without music.

Stick paper to the table and make similar wave movements as with music (see above).

Draw fish like this. Do a vertical line that is above the back of the rear fin.

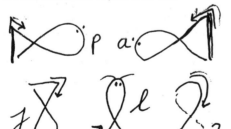

Here the children will discover the figure 2 and that helps to avoid sloppy corners.

Link the ends of the line to make a fish crossing your own line.

Draw the fins and one or two eyes and then do fish the opposite way round, draw a horizontal line and make the fish downwards, just like above but make them upwards.

Practise drawing the fish with two crayons and then again in the opposite direction.

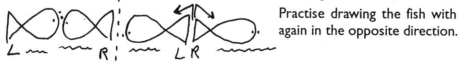

A shoal of fish, one movement but swimming in all directions, sometimes with your eyes shut or with a blind fold.

The help hand holds two fingers on the bottom line, that is the fishes bottom/back line. This represents the beginning and the end for the cross round, the other bit of the fish.

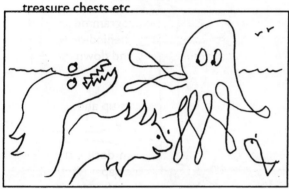

The fish exercise is a good exercise for practising links and loops over and under bits of letters. After a while the child discovers that he or she can do many different types of fish, from one line and in all directions without lifting the pen.

Let the children work on the fish shoal afterwards. Sharks with sharp teeth, fins, seaweed, wrecks, treasure chests etc.

Fill the paper with seagulls, let them have big wave shaped wings, two dots for the eyes, a sharp corner/triangle is the beak. This is an excellent exercise for later being able to leave the right amount of space between the words. The eye dots practise carefulness, attention to detail.

The silver wings, two and two.

Gradually the children can discover that there are many drawings which can be exciting to do together. This stimulates them to be considerate and work together.

Let the children sit in twos beside each other. They both shut their eyes or have blindfolds. They hold one crayon together and create water with wave movements. This is an excellent exercise for the blackboard.

Make sure that it doesn't get too stormy, let them look or perhaps even decide on a new colour and carry on with the fish. Look and choose a new colour again to do the seagulls.

Another alternative is to let them take it in turns, one child beginning with waves while the other watches.

After a while they change and the other one can now create more waves on top.

You can do a Write Dance boat with one or both hands. This seems to include the round and sharp shapes without lifting the pen.

Cut out the result and stick it onto the big "water-coloured" paper.

The Sea Rhyme

Fold the paper in the middle and stick it on to the table with blue tac. Let the children have a crayon in each hand and make this walrus picture while they are saying the rhyme. It is an old Swedish song.

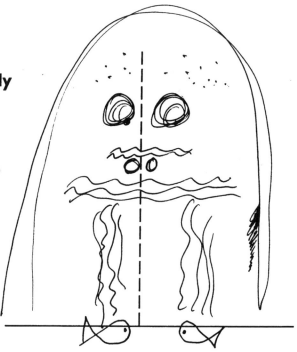

1 - **A night so cold, cold**
2 - **I steered my boat, boat, boat**
3 - **The waves went higgeldy-piggely**
3 - **Oh look, poor me, poor me!**
4 - **I stood and watched and**
     watched and watched
5 - **To wave higgeldy-piggeldy peep**
6 - **Far in the deep -**
     a - the - peep - a - the peep
7 - **I saw a fish**
8 - **And that was you!**

Structure-Wave-Movement.

Fold A4 size paper into eight sections or seven folding lines, along the long side or copy from page 22.
Put down five dots, equally distributed along the lines (see page 47-48)
Do movement circles four or five times on top of the dots.
Do wave movements around the circles and say out loud "up down up" or "over under over" or invent imaginary directions.
Repeat the wave movements on top of each other again and again.
Let the waves go back to make a whole chain and repeat it in with many colours.

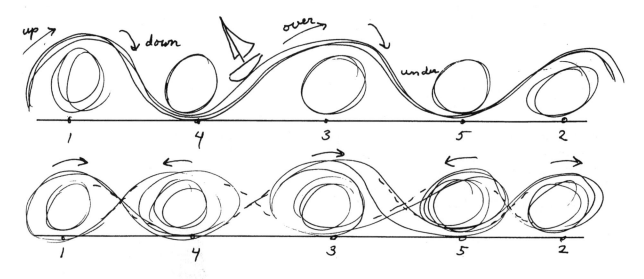

Cats

Half round backwards and forwards movements.

Talk about cats or start immediately with the music.
The music comes from the musical 'Cats'.

In this week themethe child is going to be drawing cats but it can be other animals as well.
With two pieces of chalk or crayons, one in each hand, the child is going to draw half circles backwards and forwards, inwards outwards, up, down.

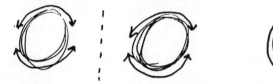

These are waves which are a difficult pen movement. This is important for joined up a, c, d and g.

Some children, more often boys than girls, have a problem with this and do pointed, open
instead of nice smooth curves (bent curves).

Use the theme 'Cats' also for other subjects. Half circles and eights are the basis for simple cat combinations which the child can develop further. This is a playful and creative way of learning round ligatures/ joins.

Gross Motor Preparation with Music

Let the children stand behind the table or spread out in the room.
Practise first without music, stretch your arms high up in the air and swing them in parallel to the right then left at the same time as the hips swing in the opposite direction.
Count one, two, one, two.
Put the music on and practise sticking your hands against your side. This is less tiring.

Cats on paper with music.

Fold a large piece of paper in the middle and stick it on the table.
In the middle of each half the child draws a dot and then big circles around it.
Make them both with inwards and outwards movements (as in the circles and eight music).

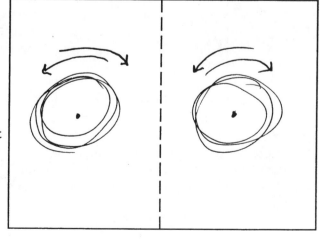

At the starting point of these circles, with a crayon in each hand, the child draws half circles with backwards and forwards movements.

Let the music lead once the children know what they want to do. Start with bows and let the hands work in parallel, in other words, with both hands at the same time doing right or left movements respectively.

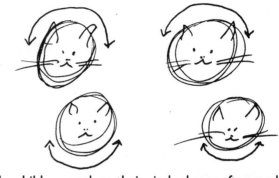

Repeat the music and now draw half circles on the lower edge of the circle shape. Listen carefully to the music and follow it.

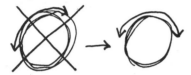

Let the children work on their circle shapes afterwards, for example, making them into cat heads. Be careful, some children don't do half circles but only quarter ones.

This is an excellent exercise to help them later on to manage links between a, c, d and g.

Other Cat Movements

Let the children play and practise round, back and forth movements a bit more. Let them create Write Dance mushrooms, boats, tunnels, fir trees and monkeys. Let the children choose if they want to use one or both hands. Fold the paper in the middle. Put a middle dot in each half.

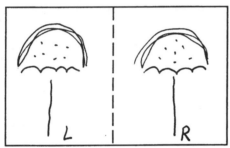

Mushrooms.

Swing your way to the hat in parallel or mirror parallel movements. The extended arcade lines become the bottom bit of the mushroom top (head/hat). The circle movements downwards build the foot.

Boats

are created in a similar way, begin with the keel.

Train tunnels

From small tunnels to big, from big to small.

Monkey

Create the eyes with circle movements. The eyebrows grow thick through repeated back and forth movements. The head and ears are created by half circle movements, a big happy mouth.

Fir trees

The important thing here is that the branches shouldn't be created with stiff movements but that they should develop external swinging in and out movements.

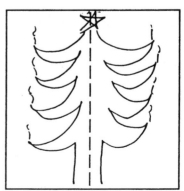

Bears (Can also be dome during circle and eights week theme).

Make the basic teddy with 13 circles, or hand it out already copied.

Join up the circles in one single '8-movement' with another colour.

Only lift the pen to do the face.

How many eights have you drawn?

Coordinated crayon and body movements

The children stand behind the table in a ring or spread out in the room (gym or play-hall).

Start down by the neck (with one or both hands), move the hand up over the head, to the nose and back again ….. a cat washing its face.

Let the children say "I'm a cat, washing itself…. Meow"! They say "meow" when their hands reach, and grasp, their noses. Now the brain can hear what the hand does.

The purpose of this exercise is for the child to understand the connection between the round movements of the hand and the round letters.

Fold a piece of A4 paper in three parallel folds and stick it to the table. On one fold, draw 5 evenly-spaced circles (see page 64). Draw rightwards-facing profiles of cats, dogs, friends, cockerels…. Put the noses / about one third of the circle.

As the help hand strokes and 'washes' the head, from neck to nose, the writing hand does just the same. First with a finger, later with a crayon.

Practise later with a pen: in reality this is a row of c's with heads and noses.

Cat-rhyme
1 - I am a cat and I am washing myself
2 - I wait and I wait and I wait
3 - Listen for the clock to strike eight
4 - A little mouse in his hole
5 - He is hiding and teasing I know
6 - Without a tempting little snack
7 - I have to turn my back.

Mandala
Combination of straight and round movements

The music (on CD) for this final week is a combination of seven pieces that we have already heard.

We're going to encourage straight and round movements. This is actually the most important part of writing, the ability to make both round and straight lines, along with being able to write quickly, personally and legibly.

When letters are joined up you need soft, rounded corners just like in the curved risers and descenders.

We can say that the letter 'l' stands with its a straight back on the line.

not like this ... but like this!

Let the children discover the l in their own bodies with a straight back. Imagine a ball resting on the foot. This is important to get them used to the idea that the corner should be slightly rounded, so that there's room for the ball.

Figures are also made up of straight and round lines. The teacer draws the figures on the blackboard. Some teachers do a 5 in one line from top to bottom. Generally the angle is done too quickly, and the 5 looks more like an S

Begin with the downstroke; then the curve: Say that the five is going to fill its

mouth with pancakes. The horizontal line represents the eyebrows:

Just like every other week, the children begin with body-movements. One explanation for why we 'write with our bodies' could be:

Our bodies work like living computers. The brain gets its 'software' through the muscles, because they send it small signals. The brain is a sort of memory. Now it can feel for example, what is straight and what is round, straight lines and 8-movements. In that way the body helps the brain. The brain helps the fingers to write and to keep the movements in our memory for the rest of our lives.

When we write, we know how we want the letters and figures to look. We can join them up nice and carefully with smooth movements.

The brain knows how they look, and how they should be formed, because the brain has been programmed with the help of the body. Smooth handwriting comes from the whole body.

We do the same when we learn to skate. Each careful movement in the beginning is programmed into the brain. After a bit of practice, the brain recognises and remembers all the complicated movements. Gradually it becomes automatic – the body has taught the brain, and now the brain teaches the body to skate fast, but smoothly and safely. You and the movement have become one.

Now you're going to draw a sun or a star which shines out in a circle. The circle is called a mandala in an Asian language and that's what this exercise is called too.

In the East adults and children draw mandalas in the sand with sticks. They decorate their houses with circles. They're beautiful and they mean different things – you can send messages to people by using different shapes of mandala.

When you throw a stone in the water it makes ripples, bigger and bigger. The stone is the centre, the origin, the start of everything.

When you draw the mandala or move your arms round you, you too are in the middle of everything. You are the centre and everything around you is growing bigger and bigger.

Gross Motor Preparations with Music

Let the children spread out round the room (you need a gym or playhall here).

This exercise is a bit complicated, so start by practising without music. The description is of the body-movements, but the illustrations show what the children draw on the board or paper (a layer at a time) to the music. Use square-shaped paper if you can.

1 African drums.
The children fling their arms out at chest-height, turning around slowly on the spot, to make a 'ray-circle'.

2 A walk in the country.
Arms and hands make wave and water movements. Turn slowly around on the spot, in the opposite direction to the previous exercise.

3 Robot.
Make sharp corners with wrists and arms.
Clench and spread your fingers.
Turn around the whole time with the rhythm and speed of the music.

Change direction now and again.

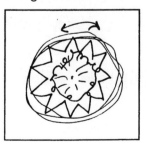

4 Circles and eights.
Stand still, one arm at a time does a half-circle, a kind of relay-race with an invisible baton which is passed on and taken up. Stretch one hand straight out in front of the body and then move it slowly behind your back, where it meets the other and then goes forward again. In front of the body it meets the first arm again and takes over the movement5 Robot.

5 Robot
- see 3

6 Silverwings
- waves with hands.

7 Train
Parallel movements beside the body - see page 50

8 Tree.
Stretch the arms out straight in arcade form, or garlands. Pick apples in the air.

Mandala on Paper or Board with Music

Use square-shaped paper if possible. Let the children try to measure out, with eyes and fingers, the middle and make a mark there. Then let them fold the paper in four equal parts (horizontally and vertically, to make a cross-fold). Is the mark right in the middle? Here they practise hand-eye coordination.

Let them stick the paper to the table with blu-tac. They make movements and lines to the music, with one or both hands (or changing around, as they like).

Draw a mandala on the board as an example. If one of the children doesn't manage to do one movement completely, let them go on to the next one and finish off later when we repeat them.

See above for which lines go with which music.

Individual Practice without Music

Big paper, preferably square. Look carefully and decide where the middle is, and put a dot there (good overview practice, and also develops a useful habit).

As above, fold in four parts and see if the mark ends up anywhere near the right place. Let each child stick a little picture of themselves in the middle

Make a frame around the picture with round and straight shapes.

Try to spread the shapes and movements as evenly over the paper as possible. You could cut the mandala out and stick it on coloured paper.

Board and Paper Games in Twos

Circles and straight

Two children sit opposite each other, or walk round the table with the paper stuck on it whilst they take turns to draw the mandala.

One child just draws straight and angular shapes, the other round and soft ones. Let them each use their own colour, to make the differences clearer.

This exercise is good practice in understanding the difference between straight and curved.

Football game

Draw a football pitch on the blackboard and let the children work there. Emily is the goalie, and Eric is the team. Decide how many players there are in the team. Eric marks them out.

Now Eric has to pass the ball between the players with looped movements. He can use one hand. Neither the goalie (who also moves around with looped movements in his goal) nor the players can stand still, but have to move around all the time with circle movements.

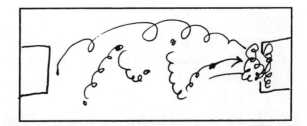

The players try to pass the ball to each other and make looped movements all the time. The trick is to shoot quickly with a stretched out movement. The goalie has to try to stop the 'ball' with his chalk, otherwise it's GOAL!

Change over.

The football game can also be played on a table with a large fixed piece of paper. The children sit opposite each other.

The game is very suitable to get rid of surplus energy. It may be best to have this as the last part of the lesson.

The football game is a challenge to make your own rules, practises adjustment and respect it.

Mandala-rhyme

A very good finger exercise which helps the brain to remember straight and round, at the same time as the eyes can see the shapes on the board. It can be hard for children at first, so take it very slowly.

2 5 6   1 - Two, five and six   2 5 5
2 - Are straight and round and straight and round
3 - Six, nine and ten
6 9 10   **4 - Where are you then?**
5 - One, four and seven
1 4 7   **6 - Are only straight, like eleven** | | |-| 7
7 - But zero, three and eight
0 3 8   **8 - Are round and sleep till late**

The teacher writes the figures on the blackboard and points to them while the children do the reading.

1 - Stretch out only the amount of fingers indicated and pointed at on the blackboard
2 - Stretch and bend all fingers
3 - Stretch out the amount of fingers and look at the blackboard
4 - Hide your face behind your hands
5 - Stretch out the amount of fingers
6 - Keep stretching out the fingers
7 - Indicate zero with think and index, then stretch out the amount of fingers
8 - Band your arms and makr rocking movements.

Carry On

... with Write Dance part I, over and over again. Even in middle school there are good reasons to practise some of the basic movements from time to time. The children won't mind, in fact, just the opposite.

In Write Dance part 2 we start to practise joined-up handwriting. Its 24 chapters don't just practise handwriting, but also the basic movements to music, though sometimes with smaller movements and more quickly. Naturally, it'll be an advantage if these children have practised on Write Dance part I, but it isn't essential.

Children with behavioural problems.

Some children always make themselves visible by being heard most, always pushing themselves forward, spoiling games or wanting to be in charge all the time, especially when it comes to new exercises. These children usually have an inner insecurity and need a fixed structure and a routine in their learning. They often behave anti-socially to attract attention to themselves.

These children often have immature handwriting, with poor rhythm and uncoordinated shapes, movements and distribution. They have little or no harmony between relaxed and excited in their behaviour.

These children often have a surplus of energy, power, vitality and aggressiveness. (the word aggressiveness comes from the Latin **agere**, which means to act. This can be both positive and negative, though the word now has a negative connotation).

Experience of using Write Dance with groups shows that these children have a chance to behave socially with Gross Motor movements in the air, but with movement exercises on paper they're fascinated at finally being allowed to move around freely. This applies especially to the Volcano, Robot, Train and the Growing Tree.

They draw with a passion and force that can sometimes tear the paper. The children are impressed at what they themselves have created. Do they perhaps see themselves in the drawings?

During the calmer themes, though, like Walk in the Country, Circles and Eights and Silver Wings, these children often get restless again. The calmer atmosphere affects them subconsciously.

The loopy animals, however, challenge this kind of child to make his imagination and inner life concrete on the writing surface. The child may draw sharp teeth and frightening details with a lot of pressure and often in black.

Of course, there are many types of 'well functioning' children who also draw sharks' teeth and 'nasty things'.

How can we help these children?

Often these children already receive extra help, such as special teaching, psychological help, or coordination exercises, but these aren't enough for their daily lives.

If you notice that a child has particular difficulty in concentrating on individual work, try the following exercise:

Fix a large piece of paper (A3, or bigger if possible) to the table or preferably the blackboard. Let the child paint with underarm movements, to and fro. You can ask the child to count up to 100, then change paints, so you end up with a cascade of different colours.

Show how the underarms can be like wings or a machine which carries on moving, even when you lift them from the paper. When the arms drop down again they carry on painting, like a robot. The child will like the machine analogy – don't try to bring feelings in here.

Demonstrate how you can count slowly, with a steady rhythm, both when the arms are in the air and on the paper – one beat for each to and fro movement.

When the writing arms are tired out, the child with surplus energy is usually pleased and admires his work, after which he may be ready for more concentrated work.

Colour in small squares (5cm) with crayons. Don't leave any of the paper uncovered. This is going to be a mosaic. Cover the whole surface with black or dark blue in big movements. Use a sharp object to scratch out shapes – the lines will show the colour from underneath.

This is a nice exercise for a larger group as well.

The football game is a good way of letting out energy, competing, winning, learning to lose, adjusting, creating rules and exercising the finger and hand muscles. Compare this with young animals' need to charge around sometimes.

Children who are shy, cautious, or slow, often just need time to 'take in' the movements, the social part of the game, the music, their own role.

The gross motor exercises can feel frightening for some children. Some bits may seem oppressive so let the child stand aside and watch for a while.
Thanks to the incredible power of music, the child will sooner or later come back in. Experience has shown that children generally feel able to take part very soon.

Combining Music with Imaginative Drawings

Infant and Junior schools can work together to compile a Write Dance programme covering several years. Children love to repeat things they know – exercises, situations, stories, feelings. It makes them feel secure. It opens the way to what Matti Bergström (Finnish professor in child psychology) calls 'the brain's cloud of possibilities'.

It's a good idea either to plan Write Dance for a set time each week or, even better, to integrate the method into as many lessons as possible.

In the Autumn term of Year 1, you'll be able to repeat all of the music drawings and the rhymes that go with them, and you should be able to fit in all the other exercises that go with each theme.

In the Spring of Year 1 you can repeat, for example, a combination of music-drawings and imaginary figures twice a month. This creates more time for variations on the themes (see the following pages).

In the Autumn term of Year 2 it's sufficient just to repeat the gross motor movements with music now and again and, instead of the music exercises with large sheets of paper, you can use smaller ones or copy books. Play around with the variations and make up your own. Challenge the children to make up movements and drawing-tasks to the songs that they know.

The story which connects all themes

Once upon a time there was a volcano. It had a big fire in its belly. One day the volcano could not hold it any longer and it threw everything out. The air was black with smoke, stones and lava. It thundered down in a big glowing river. Then came the rain and cooled everything down again.

Sometimes we feel a volcano inside our bellies. It gives tension, we feel frustrated because we cannot be angry whenever we want to be. The volcano helps you to get rid of all the cramped feelings in your body. After that you will feel relaxed, you have calmed down.

The landscape around a volcano is very fertile. People in the landscape wandered around to find a good spot to settle. Maybe it was next to the volcano. They walked in the country for days. The country teaches you to relax even more. You can close your eyes and sit or lie down. Relax and move your arms or the whole body in slow flexible movements. On paper it becomes typical 'krongelidong' movements. All sorts of animals who only live in your imagination and originate from your 'krongelidong-lines'. Therefore we call them krongelidong animals.

The people (we call them Writedance-people), started to grow plants and vegetables. They cooked them into a delicious soup while stirring them in circular movements. The women rocked their babies in sleeping eights and they fell asleep. At eight they woke up and started to work again. There were lots and lots of special flowers in the country. The writedance people did everything in curved and circular movements. We make these movements with our arms, legs, feet and with our crayons on a writing surface.

One day they got visitors. The people did not know where they came from but they called themselves robots. They could only move in a rigid and strange way. The writedance people liked this way of expression and combined then with their circled movements. The robots tried to dance together with the rocking women. They started to build houses and castles, in curved and square shaped. We make these robot movements with our whole body; on the writing surface they become stretched, straight and angled lines.

The writedance people developed all sort of machines. One of them was the train. It puffed and whistled joyfully through the country. The people started to communicate by letters which originate out of the puffing smoke. We call them arcades and garlands and we can express them in the air and on a writing surface.

The landscape transformed from time to time. One period there was a thick forest with many trees. The writedance people also cultivated fruit trees and they discovered that they could act out the trunk, the branches and the leaves by dancing to music, in the air and on paper. They discovered that there was a connection between the tree movements, the straight and bending lines and loops. We express them in the air and on paper.

They danced also to the waves of the sea and discovered the rhythm in the flight of the seagulls. It had silverwings. They acted out waves everywhere, on the rocks and in the sand. They made waves in the rails of the train they embroidered waves on their clothes. We express them in the air and on a writing surface.

At that time the cat was already a very lovable pet. The writedance people imitated his washing behaviour and they imagined all sorts of games and rhymes together. They expressed the washing cats movements to music in the air and on a writing surface. They discovered that they could add these movements to their written letters.

They were a very happy people and once year they celebrated the union of all movements and symbols in a circle or a mandala: up and down, left and right, bending, circling, flexible and straight, stretching and angled, tensing and relaxing. Sun and moon, boy and girl, father and mother, heaven and earth, fire and water..... They expressed their dancing in the air and on a writing surface. All this happened a long long time ago but their memories still live in our mind. That is why we are able to learn writing with the help of dancing... ℋ

Starting points for your own ideas

Combination of Volcano + Walk in the Country + Train + Robot

Fold a large piece of paper down the middle. Let the children create a Volcano on one half to music. Change the music and change straight over to Walk in the Country on the other half.

Let the children create imaginary figures round the Volcano and in the countryside, water, Write Dance trees…

Helped by the Train or Robot music the children will be able to frame the pictures in with arcades, garlands or angels.

Combination of circles and eights + Robot

Use squared paper if you can. Make a Clover-8 to music (lying down, standing or a Clover-flower). Frame in the picture with appropriate shapes to the Robot music.

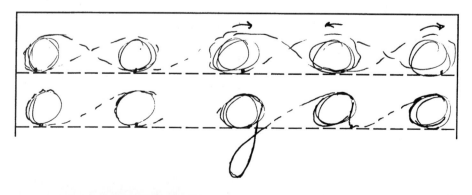

Combination of Walk in the Country + Train

Do the Walk in the Country in plough-shape (see page 54). Two chalks tied together with a rubber band can be used to draw the rails.

Play the Train music and press pause now and again to indicate a station in which the children circle around until they think of a town for the train to carry on to.

Afterwards add trains, cars, cycles.

Combination of circles and eights + Cats

Fold a sheet of A3 paper in 8 sections (see page 54). Now the children do circle-movements (see page 47-48 for division of the rows).

To the eights music or Cats (a bit faster and more difficult) the children make joined-up eights or ocean-waves. Can they also join up a, c, d, g?

Combination of the Sea + the Tree

Start by creating the sea on the lower part of the paper using as much detail as you want, but with rhythmic wave-movements.

Play the Silverwings music. Make layers of the waves: big, small…

Then let the children draw an island with a forest on it on the top half.

Finish off the picture (with or without music) with imaginary figures: seagulls, fish, little flowers (of clover-8s), monkeys, trees.

Then frame it in, perhaps, to the Robot or Train music.

Combination of Circles and eights + the Sea

Fold a sheet of A3 paper and draw 5 circles on each line.

Play the Silverwing music. Let your pen 'dance' over and under the circles on the first line then go back along the same row.

Do the same on the next row, but go back in the opposite direction to build a chain, or two snakes.

On the third row, join the circles in twos to make sleeping eights.

On the last row, do the same as the third but make standing 8s as well: make sleeping eights.

The children can finish off the pictures by colouring them in or putting animals in the circles.

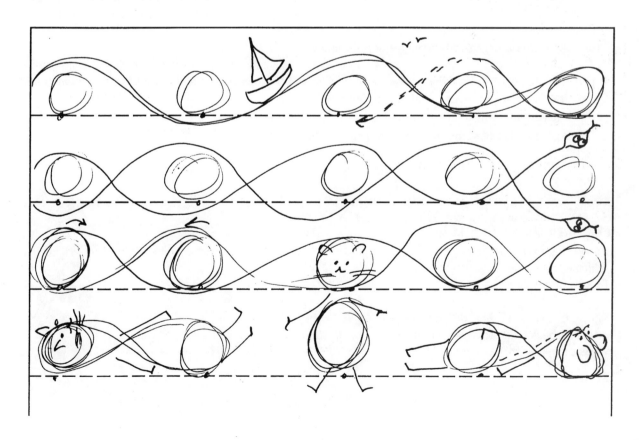

Write Dance Folding Books

(see following pages)

The children make one or two folding books which they can use at various times. They can be stuck on to their writing or maths books, to remind them of the basic writing movements of Write Dance. They can decorate their writing or maths books when they've finished a piece of work, using patterns from their folding book.

The children can ask a friend to pick a number, up to seven, then fold the paper that number of times. They then use the pattern that comes up.

- Copy both the originals for each child if they are to have two folding-books each, or just one if they are only going to have one.
- Cut along the outside
- Make sharp edges along the dotted lines. Fold each one both outwards and inwards. The children may need some help with this.
- The children draw on the back of each book the patterns from the other so that they end up with two folding books each.
- Practise folding the books in different ways; a different page will come up each time.

Blind-man's buff exercise:
Shut your eyes and fold the book. This will be a delicate sensory motor finger-game. After a little practice they'll be able to fold the book without looking.

Lectures and Inset Days

The Write Dance method is simple, practical and fun to work with for teachers, day-care staff, special education teachers and nursery staff.

Take the time to sit down, watch the video, study the material together and plan the Write Dance year ahead.

Study-days can be organised through the publishers.

If you are interested in knowing more about Write Dance please contact the publishers and we can:
- ask questions on your behalf of the author
- put you in touch with someone from the Handwriting Interest Group
- provide a list of some untranslated references.

Lucky Duck Publishing Ltd.
34 Wellington Park
Clifton
Bristol BS8 2UW

Phone or Fax 0117 9732881 or 01454 776620
e-mail publishing@luckyduck.co.uk
website www.luckyduck.co.uk

Folding Books

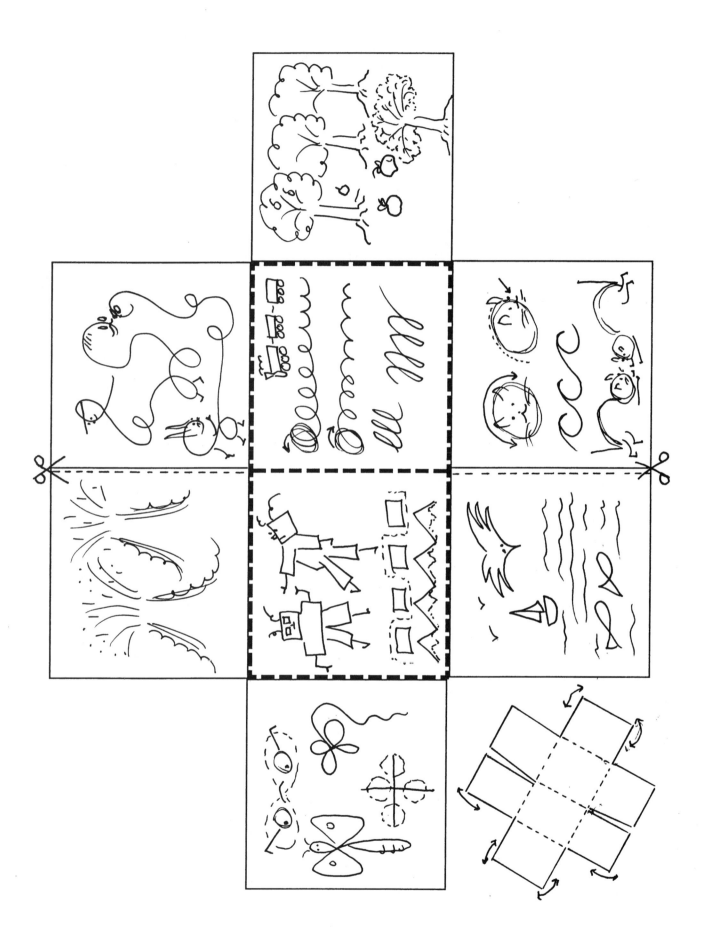

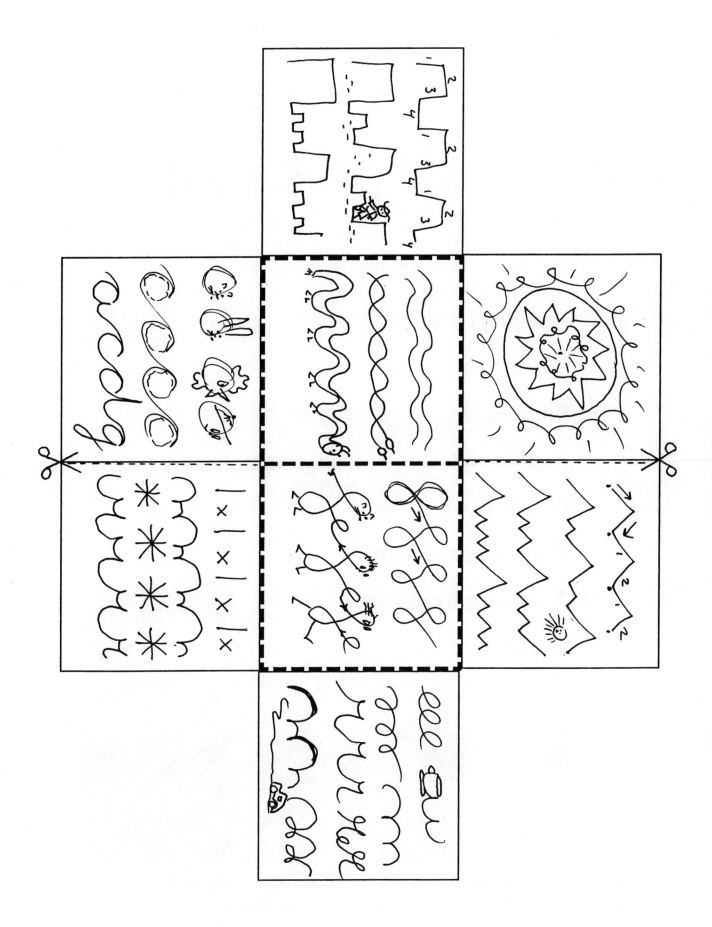

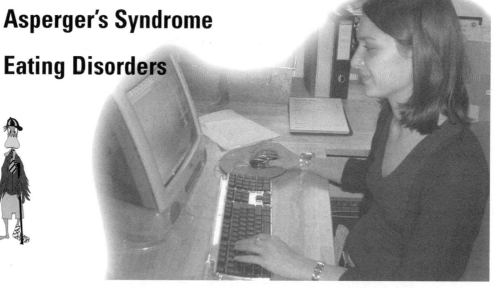